Youth Soccer Development
Progressing the Person to Improve the Player

Noel Dempsey

Oakamoor Publishing

Published in 2015 by Oakamoor Publishing, an imprint of Bennion Kearny Limited.

Copyright © Oakamoor Publishing

ISBN: 978-1-910773-13-0

All Rights Reserved. No part of this publication may be reproduced, stored in a retrieval system, or transmitted in any form or by any means, electronic, mechanical, photocopying, recording or otherwise, without the prior permission of the publisher.

This book is sold subject to the condition that it shall not, by way of trade or otherwise, be lent, re-sold, hired out or otherwise circulated without the publisher's prior consent in any form of binding or cover other than that it which it is published and without a similar condition including this condition being imposed on the subsequent purchaser.

Bennion Kearny has endeavoured to provide trademark information about all the companies and products mentioned in this book by the appropriate use of capitals. However, Bennion Kearny cannot guarantee the accuracy of this information.

Published by Oakamoor Publishing, Bennion Kearny Limited
6 Woodside
Churnet View Road
Oakamoor
Staffordshire
ST10 3AE

This book is dedicated to my wonderful partner Naomi
and our son Theo, who are the two most important people in my life.
Thank you for your love and support.

Acknowledgements

I would like to acknowledge and thank all of the people that helped me with the research, opinions, and thinking that went into this book. I would like to thank the countless coaches, academy managers, teachers, and lecturers who have taken the time to sit down and have conversations with me and shown an interest in my writing. Your words have been the basis of this book, so thank you for that.

I would like to pay special thanks to Joel Kerr and Jamie Fullarton, whose chats have been an inspiration. They have helped shape the type of person, teacher and coach I want to be. Also, I would like to thank Mark Edwards, a friend and colleague who has helped guide me down my coaching and teaching path since we met three years ago.

Finally, I would like to thank Jack Trainer, an inspiring man who – through countless coffee meetings and conversations – has enlightened me with his knowledge and experience. They are invaluable and have helped shape my thought processes.

Noel Dempsey

Originally from London, now based in Manchester, Noel Dempsey has lived and worked within the North-West for the last three-and-a-half years during which time his journey within football coaching and education has taken off. He is currently an academy coach with the Youth Development Phase at an English Championship club.

Noel has been fortunate to work within a number of professional football clubs both as a coach and as a teacher and is currently in the process of completing his UEFA A license with the English Football Association. He has already completed the FA Youth Award.

Noel is also a qualified teacher with a Degree in Sport Science and a Master's Degree in Sport and Exercise Psychology. He has worked in a range of mainstream educational establishments over the years within Further Education, and more recently in Secondary Education.

Table of Contents

1. What's been done in the past? And how it impacts on the present and future	1
2. The curse of the 'Boys Club'- a factor in the development of young English players	7
3. Combating the Development Issue - Core vs. Youth Pathways	15
4. General Approaches to Coaching	23
5. Methods of teaching, training and coaching	33
6. Things to think about	53
7. Developing the person - Why is this just as important?	63
8. Does talent exist? Are we pigeon-holing people?	69
9. How mainstream education affects us developing the person	75
10. Academic Education vs. Life Education	83
11. How we learn	89
12. Must nurture; Do not leave it to nature	97
13. Having a core set of beliefs and values	103
14. Instilling Confidence	113
15. Motivation - An Environment Built Around Players	117
16. Family, and Friends - How they affect players	125
17. Developing your own Environment for Success	129
Epilogue	135

1. What's been done in the past? And how it impacts on the present and future

The roots of our Soccer Tribe lie deep in our primeval past. Desmond John Morris

Without delving into the depths of football's history (which would undoubtedly take up an entire book by itself) this first chapter aims to offer a concise look at what may have contributed to the lack of quality young players being developed in England for the past few decades.

It must be made clear that there is no 'one' factor that has resulted in the decline of quality players coming through the English academy system; instead it has been a number of key factors, over a prolonged period of time, that has contributed to England's downfall.

The Charles Hughes era

The majority of us who coach are likely to be familiar with the name of Charles Hughes, the English coach turned head of coaching at the F.A. whose tactics have caused great debates over the past few decades over his so called 'long ball tactics'. The quote below came from a report published in *The Independent* newspaper and highlights what Hughes was looking for in his teams.

"Hughes, like Taylor, believes in the accurate long pass and points to great teams whose most significant goals have come from five passes or fewer. In upholding the concept of using the accurate long pass as a legitimate tactic, Hughes is in good company. The late Arthur Rowe, architect of Tottenham's aesthetically attractive push and run, once said: 'If I had players who could kick the ball with accurate precision 50 yards all the time, I would use them.'"

Many have criticised Hughes' style of coaching, many more have blamed him for the distinct lack of creativity that he seemingly created across the F.A. and the way in which coach educators were instilling Hughes' principles into (what was then) the new generation of coaches. Since then, the English game has been plagued with what is now seen as 'old school' coaches who simply ask their players to smash the ball long.

Although we can see potential issues with this tactic now (though that is not to say we do not still use it and use it to great effect!) it was not necessarily the worst tactic to adopt at the time. Consider a range of factors that players and coaches would have had to deal with; think of the playing surfaces, the design of the balls, and the boots, and what initially seems such a poor tactic turns into one we can potentially understand (although it still doesn't have to be accepted of course!).

It got me thinking about what was required to help develop our young players and something clicked when I recently attended a workshop run by the Football Association, which was related to systems of play. Whilst discussing a particular formation (4-4-2) a jolly looking fellow, who had seemingly been coaching for a number of years said to the group '4-4-2 is ingrained in our English culture of playing, it is what we have grown up with'.

That was it! For me the penny dropped and for the first time I could see the real issue. It wasn't the tactic that was important; it could have been any tactic or any style of play. The problem was that we as a nation were 'ingrained' in the wrong style of *coaching*. Simple enough for most to figure out, I am sure, but what struck a particular chord was that no one had discussed the player as a person and how that person should be developed. This seemed true as much today, as it was in the time of Hughes.

In the Hughes era - the *player* needed to be developed; the *player* had to be ingrained in a system. But the person? Well, not a lot was said about the person really. In fact, within the coach education set up at that time there was no real focus on the person at all. That era of coach education was about creating coaches who were geared to coach a system, not a player and not a person. The coach was not educated to put his own ideas into action.

The unfortunate thing now is that these coaches still exist and are still educating others. It is not so much a philosophy that they are trying to teach, simply a system of play, and with that system being 'ingrained' into coaches and therefore into players – it takes away much of the 'personal' development from that player.

It is removing choice, removing decision making and freedom to play, and instead instilling a numb outdated tactic that is simply insufficient for youth players today. It does not match the game's demands, it does not fit into society, into education and learning, and it offers nothing in the development of the person.

How the F.A. and Premier League tried to change the fortunes of the English game

The Charter for Quality

With the production of young homegrown players in decline, the F.A. brought in Howard Wilkinson to investigate and shake things up.

'The Charter for Quality' was published in 1997 and it outlined a range of ideas including the introduction of a select range of elite academies that would contain all the best players in the country (together in a close set up) to allow for the best development to take place. This idea was one of many but, as so often within the English game, much of what was proposed ended up either not happening, or being diluted so much that the desired effect was never really seen.

Wilkinson was a breakthrough, though, and he recognised the importance of youth development and the creation of a philosophy that would reap the rewards in years to come. The charter has ultimately now been lost in its own translation and although it has undoubtedly contributed to the development of other more recent initiatives, it would appear that these types of reports/studies/investigations (or whatever you want to call them) continue to be produced to seemingly tackle the same issue(s) in a different way!

Having enrolled onto one of the League Managers Association courses myself – which Howard Wilkinson contributes to – I can see what he was looking for from his Charter. He offered excellent suggestions on the importance of contact time for coaches and players to train together, to have academies take preference over school sports, and to have more 'quality time' in matches rather than quantity.

However, there were still key factors missing and mistakes made that hurt what Wilkinson had set out to do. Quoted below were some of the fundamental issues that meant England was still looking for a better way to develop its youth. Wilkinson explained:

"I only envisaged 12 to 14 academies, but we finished up with 40, which in my humble opinion was always too many. I didn't think the country had enough talent to support 40 high-level development centres.

"A lot of clubs and a lot of clubs' directors would ask 'Where's our Rooney? Where's our Joe Cole?' That's how they actually judged it. The notion that 40 academies can unearth 40 Rooneys every season is unreal – it won't happen.

"The second thing was that there has to be adherence to rules. It's fair to say that there wasn't. The high standards set out in the Charter were not adhered to in some cases, in terms of numbers of coaches, the number of medical staff and education provisions and so on."

The Elite Player Performance Plan

Following Wilkinson's charter, we as a footballing nation, have tried to stop the rot through the introduction of the Elite Player Performance Plan (EPPP). In October 2011, the EPPP's overall focus was on getting more homegrown players playing regular first team football at the highest level.

At its core, the EPPP wanted to look at improving the following:

1. Increase the number and quality of homegrown players gaining professional contracts in clubs and playing first-team football at the highest level.
2. Create more time for players to play and be coached.
3. Improve coaching provision.
4. Implement a system of effective measurement and quality assurance.

5. Positively influence strategic investment into the Academy System, demonstrating value for money.
6. Seek to implement significant gains in every aspect of player development.

To meet these six main principles the Premier League wanted to focus on four areas, in particular, that they felt were of great importance. These were:

1. Coaching
2. Classification
3. Compensation
4. Education

My original excitement when reading the EPPP was the collective capacity of bringing 'coaching' to the forefront of development. In fact, the mention of 'education' gave me tingles. I thought that this document would bring together the creation and development of the long-term player development model (LTPD) and youth modules to offer some fascinating insight into how best to educate and train our youth players.

I mean the potential was there! Educating coaches to educate the player and the person, this was the opportunity for the F.A. to show they knew what was missing. They would demonstrate their understanding of our rapidly changing society, be in line with educational understanding in schools, give coaches the tools to not only be a coach but to nurture and mentor players and people. Unfortunately, this never happened.

The EPPP appeared to offer so much that many in football were excited about, including myself. That was until many clubs started going through the process of completing an audit. Moving away from the basic issues that have been highlighted by so many in football, the EPPP *does not* provide a sound base to kick-start the education of youth development. The EPPP is not designed for the education of players nor the person. Instead, it seems to be a tiring process of creating and generating paperwork and justification, about what clubs do, for external auditors that have nothing but a checklist to go from. Ticking lots of boxes determines whether or not a club reaches a particular category status. Some of these boxes might be very difficult to obtain due to the financial restrictions clubs have thanks to a lack of funding that often means they have to look for ways to raise funds to secure facilities (that may not even be the best for what they are trying to achieve). However, because this is a prerequisite for obtaining a particular status, and in order to tick the auditors' box, clubs are simply finding a facility to call their own

Although appearing to want the right things, the Premier League has created a process that is effectively, in my opinion, a waste of time. It was a 100+ page document that ultimately told us what we already knew. The EPPP appears to be a money making scheme, highlighting that clubs must have coaches obtaining as many different qualifications as possible in order for auditors to place another tick in an apparent 'important' tick box. It becomes a moneymaking system at a time when there is a desperate fight to obtain money, certainly within the lower leagues.

The F.A. Commission Report

More recently, the F.A. created a commission to further investigate the development of homegrown players. Published in May 2014 the commission identified four key problems that we are apparently facing. They were:

1. (Most importantly) inadequate competitive playing opportunities for 18-21 year old elite players at top clubs.
2. The ineffectiveness of the regulations of the player market in preserving the desired balance between English, EU, and non-EU players.
3. The quality and impact of coaching and coach education especially in grassroots football.
4. The quantity and quality of grassroots facilities, especially all weather pitches.

Now, out of the four main problems highlighted, the two main areas that can be controlled by the F.A. (options three and four in my view) have been overlooked in the first report. Stating that problems three and four would be put into a subsequent report and published in the Autumn of 2014, the F.A. chose to focus their attention on two areas that they seemingly have a lot more work to do on, and which could still result in very little gain to the development of young players. Again, like the EPPP, many of us could write entire books on the shortcomings of this report but it stands in plain sight that, once again, the F.A. are not sorting out their own glasshouse but throwing stones (pardon the vague expression) at others. The F.A.'s focus should be on coaches, their education and providing a range of suitable facilities throughout the country to allow, first and foremost, a revolution in player development to be kick-started.

The commission's seemingly huge step backwards takes away from the importance of what we need to be focusing on, which is to improve our youth players' ability to play in the game today. In order to do this, the player and the person have to be educated in the 'business' as well as the game of football. This means the *person* needs to be educated to understand the pressures, the money, the fame, commitments, agents, business models, contracts, social media. None of which are learnt on the training field and all of which can adversely affect a player's contract and career in less than a day. If players need to be educated in these areas, coaches need to be educated in these areas. The development and change to the game is so apparent that universities are now even offering postgraduate courses in 'sports directorships'; the demand for understanding both sides of the game is so great that other organisations are capitalising on it. Yet the F.A. is failing to see what is required to make an outstanding player in this country.

What will the future hold?

So we arrive at the present, having learnt that we coach predominantly the wrong style of football and have been doing so for 40 years. We have a category system in place that effectively has no real influence on youth development in this country and the F.A. are currently spending more time looking at secondary issues rather than development. It all sounds rather bleak when put into that context. For all the initiatives, reports and discussions by the 'powers that be', there is very little the worker ants on the ground can do to influence what comes out of each report or study. Instead, the focus of coaches needs to be on what *we can do* to influence the players of today and how we can make a positive impact on the players that we meet and train.

For this to happen, coaches must look to develop their own education in a number of different ways. Coaches must be mentors, must be educators, and facilitators. We must be able to speak to the person as much as we do to the player. What the future must hold – for our youth to stand any chance of making any real unique development in this country – is the development of the 'whole' game. That means a knowledge of the techniques, tactics and skills just isn't enough anymore. We, as a nation, must be the first to look beyond what is done on the field, in the gym, or in a sport psychologist's sessions. We must develop the person to meet the demands of the game while studying and learning how to play.

2. The curse of the 'Boys Club'- a factor in the development of young English players

What's the 'boys club' then?

Our national game is one we all admire and look up to. Year after year, we cannot wait for the start of the football league season, to watch some of our most beloved players take to the field; year after year, we are thrilled. But what happens when those players reach the end of their illustrious playing careers and retire, how do we then feel when we see these great players become the head coaches/managers of clubs? And as coaches, how do we feel about (and see) these ex-players when many of them do not succeed as managers?

Football is a unique industry in that the playing servants of the game will often be reintroduced to it in a different capacity when they stop taking to the field. A capacity that is effectively seen as a continuation of what they did on the park – due to the fact that the environment is the same, and the game is the same. It has been the mistake of many clubs to think in this way. The difference between playing and coaching is vast, however. So vast that it can often put off many ex-players. The point is that we see too many players being put into coaching roles with very little other than experience behind them. Surely, this needs to be addressed if we are serious about making a positive start to changing the way we develop our young generation of players.

How could these coaches impact on the person and the player?

We have all heard the saying that 'you can't buy experience' and this is true, but it is what you do with that experience that counts more. Potentially, many ex-professional players have a fantastic opportunity to use their own experiences to shape the future for others in a very nurturing and positive way. The impact that some coaches can have on youth players is huge and it is this aspect that makes clubs sign up, or re-sign, ex-professional players.

The kind of impact we want and expect from these individuals is insight into the professional world of football from a very personal perspective. These insights can be communicated to youth players to allow them to adapt and progress in similar (or sometimes completely different) ways based on what the ex-professional has come up against. It would be expected that a lot of a players' development wouldn't necessarily come in the form of technical and tactical improvement on the pitch, but instead, from conversations, team talks, and one-to-ones. You'd expect the ex-professional to offer guidance into the development of a player's psychological state, social set up, their home life, and the environment they create for themselves and others around them.

What ex-professional players have to offer in abundance is some outstanding lifestyle tales, and psychological experience, of how to be successful and sustain a career in the professional game.

So, what's the issue?

Examples of ex-footballers getting jobs in football is commonplace. There is a recent (and widely reported) example of James Beattie, the former Everton and Southampton forward who became the manager of League Two Accrington Stanley being potentially fined, along with his club, because Beattie had failed to secure a UEFA 'B' coaching licence. In the end, Beattie obtained his coaching qualification just before a £15,000 fine was due to come into effect.

As well as being an embarrassing story, it is a depressing reality that coaches have been faced with in England for a number of generations. Considering, at the time, that England had around 9,500 coaches who had achieved the necessary award (UEFA B), why was the job given to Beattie? Why was a League 2 management position given to an ex-player with no qualifications or experience in coaching?

More broadly, though, 9,500 qualified coaches in England, when compared to other major countries around Europe is cringe-worthy. Consider that Italy has just under 38,000 coaches holding a UEFA B license. France and Germany are two other nations that we are behind with 12,000 and nearly 22,000 coaches UEFA B coaches respectively. Spain, however, have roughly the same number of B license coaches as we do in England, yet they have got more than ten times the number of UEFA A license coaches with figures hitting over 13,000 as of October 2013. The Football Association has always (seemingly) sent out the message to grassroots coaches to build from the bottom and obtain the necessary experience. The F.A. has suggested that this pathway will gradually build up a coach's armoury of coaching skills, practices and qualifications. However, it seems as though the coaching pathway is lost to those who have played the game at a professional level. But why?

It is often highlighted that ex-players have obtained the 'experience' of playing the game at the highest level and that experience is enough. However, if you have had the experience of playing out-dated football from old school coaches in a game that has been transformed massively in the last decade, are you really the best person for the job? Would you give someone the job of teaching in a school or college because they have been a student? Of course not! Teachers are required to attend University and complete a degree, as well as a Post Graduate Certificate/Diploma in Education; they need to show that they are competent at their job. Even then, however, that is always not enough and certainly no guarantee that anyone would develop into being a good teacher.

So why on earth are ex-players allowed to coach at top clubs with no qualifications or experience of coaching? Where's their development? Where's their coaching pathway? I do not know many ex-players that have a Level 2 or even Level 1 award. Instead, the FA (through the PFA) has created its very own courses designed for ex-players to jump straight onto UEFA B and A licenses to enable them to meet the new EPPP standards – allowing them to get the top jobs in the country.

Tim Sherwood, unfortunately fell into this trap. He was made the Tottenham manager and sacked after just 6 months into an 18-month contract. Sherwood had taken the relevant F.A. courses, gaining his 'A license' and - despite his behind-the-scenes development in coaching and long playing experience – did not fulfil the club's expectations. On hearing that he had lost his job, I could think of only one thing, the obvious underlying reason for his departure: it was his lack of 'experience' as a manager. Now at Aston Villa, who's to say that Sherwood will be a success? Credit to him, he appears to be an honest person who has worked to gain the badges available to him and develop his coaching philosophy to fulfil the role. The question is: how long will the club give him to demonstrate that he is now a good manager and not just an ex-player? This Sherwood episode speaks volumes and neatly demonstrates the concept of the 'boys club'. Clubs are quick to retain and find roles for ex-players - thinking they can benefit from someone's experience of playing when (as evidenced here) even the right type of playing experience matched with the right qualifications, is still not enough to keep someone in the job. It demonstrates that all the playing experience in the world still cannot prepare someone for what is realistically a completely new role within football. This is where the pathway for ex-players is fundamentally wrong.

It is important that the key organisations within football see and recognise this. It seems that far too many ex-players are molly-coddled by the F.A. as footballers often leave the game not having attained other educational or vocational qualifications. They are almost stuck in what to do next!

The League Managers Association does provide funding for players to go out and obtain qualifications. However, the majority of the qualifications and opportunities they help players to attain are geared towards the football industry and coaching (others toward fitness more often than not). Thus, it is not always the fault of ex-players – they are often 'steered' into footballing capacities.

Jobs for the boys means that we, as a nation, may have missed out on some outstanding coaches who have lost interest in the game, or who have accepted the fact that they will never 'make it'. They continue to coach at the foundations of English football (which isn't always a bad thing, of course). However no one wants to be in a position where they see little reward or progression for doing something they love and are good at.

The silver linings

Despite the worrying signs into the lack of appropriate coach education pathways for ex-players, there are always examples of individuals where the correct coaching pathway can provide the right kind of foundation to becoming a very successful coach. It is this foundation that many have missed out on and, as such, essential elements of being a modern coach are overlooked; new experiences are not learnt from.

When talking about the kind of coaches that have demonstrated the importance of the right education, one *really* stands out: Jose Mourinho. The Portuguese master tactician built his coaching portfolio by completing the essential courses and being mentored by the likes of Sir Bobby Robson and Louis van Gaal. His thorough approach to the game, matched with his distinctly unique personality, has spearheaded Mourinho into world football and since 2004, his coaching career has been one of envy for many.

However, his coaching education was not fast tracked; he worked his way through and up the coaching ladder before being given a chance to become a manager. His apparent lack of playing experience has never once been brought into question since he burst onto the scene with FC Porto. Yet it was the years previous to this that were most important for Mourinho. His education in different European countries provided him with the foundation to understand the game at a deeper level, and his mentors provided him with effective support to give Mourinho all the experience he would need to succeed. Like Arrigo Sacchi, Jose Mourinho proved that you didn't have to have played the game at the top level in order to become a great coach.

It was no real surprise to see another coach – Andre Villas-Boas – come through the ranks like Mourinho. Having never played the game, Villas-Boas took up the role of opposition scout at Chelsea under the guidance of Mourinho and very quickly propelled himself into the coaching limelight (again like Mourinho). Villas-Boas was given a chance at FC Porto where he had great success, winning four trophies in one season, and he quickly became one of the most sought after coaches in Europe. Unfortunately, Villas-Boas has not, as yet, fulfilled his potential as a coach. His decision to go and coach in Russia may provide him with the experiences he feels he has to learn in order to be a top European coach. Perhaps, at present, Villas-Boas lacks the correct managerial skills, experience and/or leadership required for top European club management. Regardless of this, Villas-Boas demonstrated what could be done as a coach, whether you have played the game or not.

There have also been countless more success stories of coaches coming through the ranks in the right way. Paul Clement, the former number two to Carlo Ancelotti, is one of those major successes. The ex-Physical Education teacher worked his way up the coaching ladder and became an assistant to one of the best managers in the world, working with some of the best players in the world. In a report by *The*

Independent, Ancelotti described Clement as "one of the most dynamic and intelligent coaches with whom he has worked with".

Clement like others did not play at the professional level and instead began his coaching career early alongside his teaching, which he describes as an integral part of his development as a coach: "Teaching gave me a foundation: organisation, planning, using different learning styles and needs, the importance of good communication". His education was matched by his willingness to travel and learn. Before getting his first full time role at Fulham (within the Education and Welfare department) Clement worked at grassroots level as well as in the centre of excellence at Chelsea FC and Aston Villa. He completed his UEFA 'A' license with the likes of Brendan Rodgers and has worked with the likes of Ancelotti and Zidane. It has been some 20 years of education – learning, adapting, and expressing his views – that has enabled Clement to get to where he is. There is no doubt that Paul Clement is the epitome of an innovative, modern day football coach who has now been given his opportunity to manage in the English game (good luck to him!).

Another young coach who was shot into the limelight of professional football is Helena Costa. Appointed head coach of French Ligue 2 side Clermont Foot 63 and making football history, Costa was the first woman to be appointed as the head coach of a professional men's team, ushering in a possible new era of coaching appointments across Europe. Like Paul Clement, the sport science graduate took her coaching education seriously, working at a number of clubs (including Celtic, and Benfica's youth academy), and countries such as Qatar and Iran. Many coaches around Europe would be honoured to have such an education.

Although the appointment caused a stir in the world of football, it was potentially the beginning of a change in football. As *The Independent* stated, "It helps tackle the 'old boys' networks currently controlling the game". Although Costa has a long way to go in order to be taken seriously in the men's game, it was a positive appointment and one that Arsene Wenger supports:

"I like it," he said. "There are men managing women, why should women not manage men?

"The only thing I was always a big defender of in my life is to defend competence. If you are competent, you get the job anywhere.

"Having looked at her experience, the only restrictions you could have is she has very little experience as a coach but maybe she has top qualities and will show that.

"It's good that girls have a chance to manage men, so why not?"

Unfortunately, Costa's reign at the Ligue 2 side only lasted a matter of weeks before she walked out. She said that that events were being created without her knowledge. She explained, "There were a series of events that no trainer would tolerate and a total lack of respect as well as amateurism." Maybe the 'boys club' wasn't ready to take orders from a well-educated, top level coach (go figure…).

Do not get caught in the 'what was'

A major area of development, that a lot of ex-players find difficult, is adapting and expanding upon what players have done before. Many ex-players will still put coaching sessions on (as coaches themselves) that they went through during their playing days. Although there are some timeless classics when it comes to sessions, it is imperative coaches create sessions that stretch and challenge today's players. Many people find this easier than others and speaking to a number of colleagues within the game, a lot struggle to create their own unique sessions for what they want to see from their new players.

I myself was brought up on the foundations of physical fitness over technique. Playing as a wing back I spent most of my time shuttle running up and down the pitch to gain 'the necessary fitness to play the game' as one of my coaches told me. This was an era of coaching that should really now be obsolete, yet I still see many coaches in the professional game overthinking fitness and overlooking technique. And why do they do this? Because it is what they did as players, and they were professionals, so it must work!

Ultimately, one huge advantage I feel coaches that never played the game at professional level sometimes have is that they never got bogged down with one way of learning. There is ultimately no 'one' right way of doing something, especially in football; there are endless possibilities to try something new and for so many things to work on the field.

The importance of re-educating the person, not the ex-professional

As well as trying to create a new breed of coach from ex-professionals, it is also important to educate them as people. Football is a very closed-off industry where behaviours, language and habits are kept tightly ingrained in the system. This often leads to developments and new methods in education being overlooked and undervalued by the majority.

Football has missed out on so many areas that now have a huge impact on the development of youth players. For example, the potential of an ex-professional acting as a mentor can have huge effects on both the young player and person, but being a mentor isn't simply telling them what they did in the past and how they behaved - it is about shaping the person, and giving them guidance on key issues. As coaches, we have the job of helping develop fundamental aspects to a person's personality; aspects that they will carry for the rest of their lives. The last thing we should be telling them is what we did back in the day.

Consider the following areas and topics that we can have an impact on:

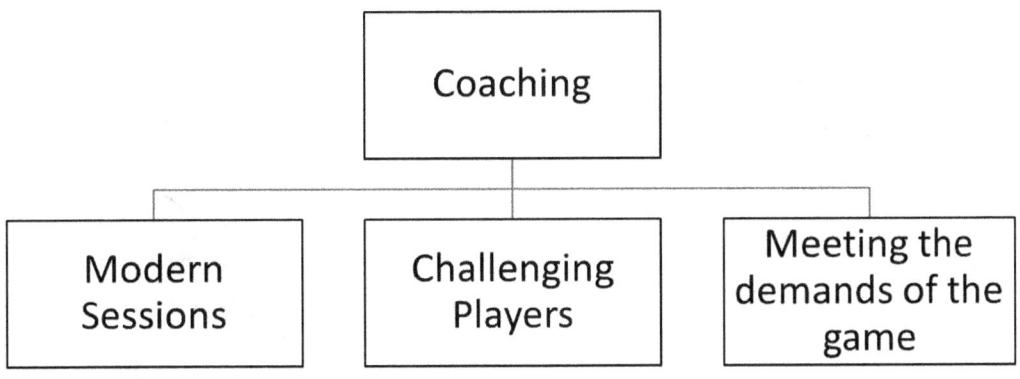

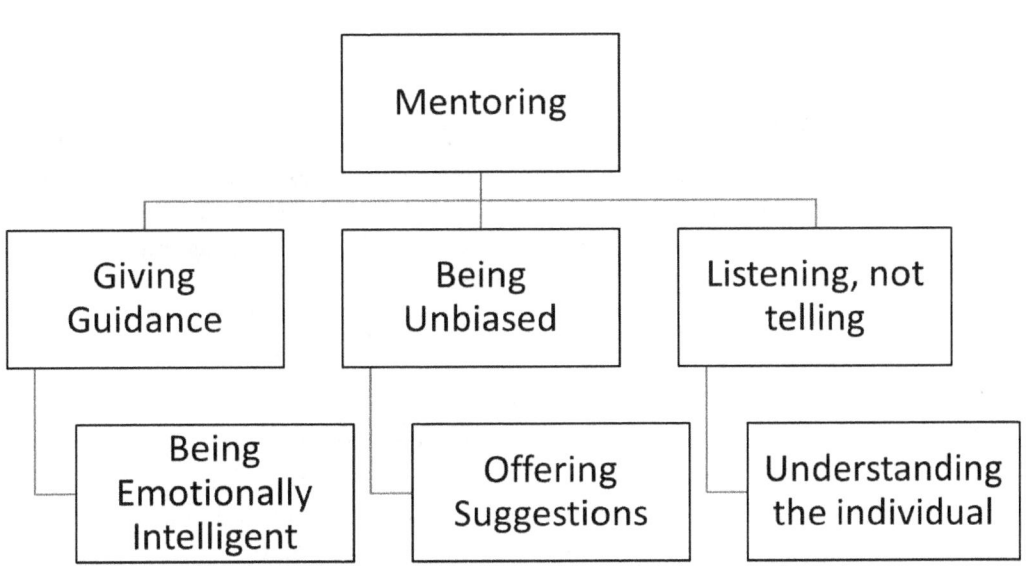

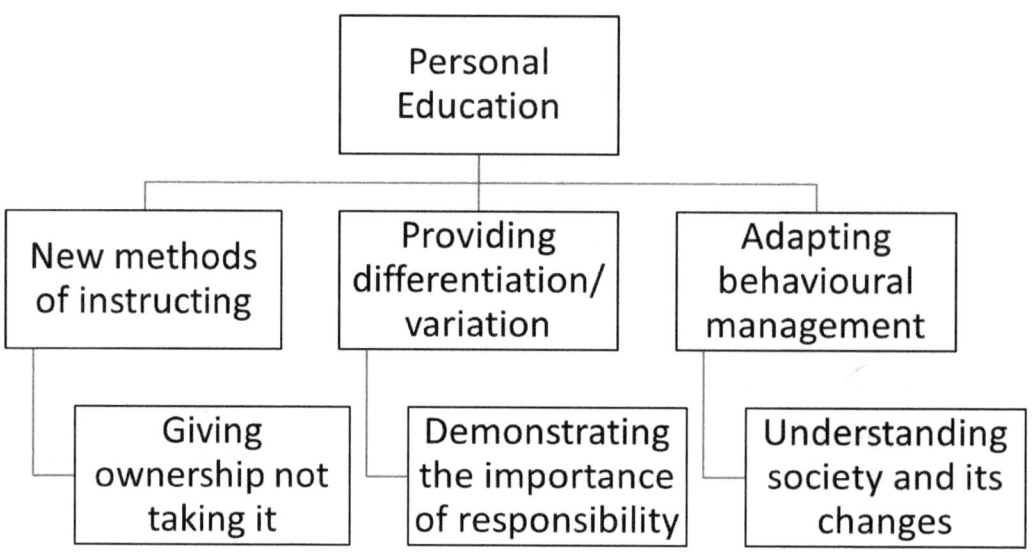

For the ex-professional, the 'coaching' element may not need that much education; it is within the 'mentoring' and 'personal education' elements where I feel ex-professionals are often caught short. These are the areas where there is so much potential to help develop the young player and person.

Summary

You can't be a pilot just because you've been a passenger.

Playing experience is a wonderful thing to have. However, experience is only one element of what is needed to coach and develop young players. Clubs need to understand that parachuting former players into coaching and management roles without them learning how to be coaches and managers (and often *over time*) is in no-one's best interests. Clubs need to understand that they should find the best coaches and managers, regardless of their backgrounds, if they want to develop the best players and teams they can.

Paul Clement has demonstrated the value of the right type of education and learning. It has paid off in the best of ways, and it is no surprise that he has excelled as Carlo Ancelotti's number two and now has the opportunity to manage after an extensive coach education period. In the next chapter, we will be looking at the traditional courses that the F.A. has provided us with, comparing them to the newer Youth Modules, and discussing how these two sets of courses look to develop the youth player and person.

3. Combating the Development Issue – Core vs. Youth Pathways

Success is no accident. It is hard work, perseverance, learning, studying, sacrifice and most of all, love of what you are doing or learning to do. Edson Arantes do Nascimento (better known as Pelé)

With the increased publicity and associated pressure on English football to develop top young players, the F.A. has spent a considerable amount of time, money and resources looking to revamp the area of coach education. From its 'Developing world class coaches and players' document released in 2008, which outlined a four year process to increase the number, and improve the quality, of coaches in England we have seen a lot of change in how we, as coaches, are being educated and developed. Although that deadline has passed now and the results of that report are somewhat mixed, there has undoubtedly been some change coming from the F.A. in how we coach our youngsters.

From the opening of St George's Park, to the reshuffling of the coaching pathway, the removal of courses, and the inclusion of new courses such as Futsal, it is safe to say that one of the biggest changes to have occurred was the introduction of the F.A. Youth Coaching Pathway (certainly in comparison to the Core Coaching Pathway courses). The Youth Pathway was designed to be able to deal with, and educate, a new generation of player, taking on-board new methods and approaches to coaching and development. The big questions this revamp threw up were:

1. Was the F.A. accepting that traditional courses were outdated and needed to be changed?
2. Were these Youth Modules eventually going to replace the more traditional courses?

Traditional Courses – What good have they done us?

STOP, STAND STILL! The three words in every English coach's armoury. Ingrained through numerous core coaching courses, these words have been part of the spine of the English coach's education pathway for a number of years.

Having completed a number of these courses several years ago and had the distinct pleasure (and I believe advantage) of attending these courses in different parts of the country - I believe they offer coaches the necessary tools to succeed. However, there are a number of key limitations to these types of courses that I believe affect the development of young players in the game today.

Strengths of these courses

Structure – for new coaches at the grassroots level, the core coaching courses provide the basic structure of how to set up a session. Unfortunately, this key organisation doesn't seem to arrive until level 2 qualifications, with level 1 only really introducing a range of fundamental games and drills (isolation). Nonetheless, from level 2 we are provided with a basic structure of how to set up a session, which is as follows:

- Warm up
- technical practice (unopposed)
- skill based practice (opposed)
- game related practice
- cool down

This structure appears simple and effective, especially for new coaches who have yet to come to grips with timings, or who may be confused with how to teach and instruct. It allows coaches to give their players an outline of what we are trying to get them to achieve in the session (as long as goals are set out beforehand).

Logical approach to coaching – many coaches will be familiar with 'on the ball, around the ball and away from the ball', and the core coaching courses provide this essential and logical tool to affect the practice, and aid players to understand particular topics that we have set out. If coaches want to work on decision making with the football, we may then need to demonstrate, instruct and guide players around the ball concerning movements to provide options, overloads, or decoys. In turn, we may then need to work on team shape meaning that we then have to move away from the ball and focus on those players (and how they can affect the play during the session with their communication and movement to become a potential option on the pitch).

Basic range of types of practices – on core coaching courses, coaches are introduced to a range of practices that can be applied to the aforementioned session structure. The key concepts of functions and phases of play provide coaches with ideas that focus on specific areas of play that we can influence. Furthermore, small sided games (SSG) offer a more game-realistic approach to a topic. The unfortunate thing is that these practices aren't brought into play until the level 3/UEFA B coaching course. More recent courses offered at St George's Park have included wave practices, squad practices and advanced technical sessions to try to meet the demands of the game.

Key Limitations that restrict the development of players today

One-dimensional – I guess this is a little bit of an unfair criticism as, seemingly, it is down to the coach to create a vibrant and multidimensional game-specific, challenging session. But, from a personal perspective, it always felt that the core coaching courses taught you in a very one-dimensional *'do it this way'* kind of way. At the beginning, I felt that my coaching style was dictated by the coach educators and it was either their way or the highway (so to speak).

This one-dimensionality gives a lot of coaches a certain amount of fear when coaching and probably restricts the creativity and confidence many would normally work with. Ultimately, this feeds through to players, stifling creativity and subsequently affecting the development of the coach and players alike. A colleague described the core coaching course final assessments as 'a driving test where you need to demonstrate the necessary knowledge and structure the way the F.A. wants to see it.'

Coach led – a big issue with this type of coaching course is that the main focus is generally put on the coach. The concept of 'Stop Stand Still' means that the coach is taking centre stage and players are often left standing around and listening (especially those away from the ball). Here players typically switch off and the message is often lost. No real substitute for this method is presented during these courses and it is often the only way of coaching that is presented.

Forgotten aspects - The introduction to the four corner model seems a wasted effort in the sense that, due to the nature of the courses, *very little* focus and time is spent on the physical and social aspect of learning. I remember, from my level 2 and UEFA B license, only spending an hour or two on these aspects. Effectively coaches were not provided with the best information on how they could develop their players and people.

What do the core coaching courses give the coach to give to the player and person?

These courses, no doubt, have their place within the coach education pathway, and there is always value in them for the simple reason that they provide a basic foundation and structure to plan and implement sessions.

However, ultimately the biggest area that needs to be recognised by both the F.A. and coaches in general is not taking everything the coach educators say as the 'be all and end all' to coaching. A distinguished colleague of mine – Jack Trainer, who is one of the most influential coach educators in the North West for the F.A. – has regularly stated that *'you must be your own person, be unique in what you do'*.

A major criticism of F.A. coach education is that it tries to produce clones. The F.A. wants us coaching their way or we will fail, but this is not the thought of many. Jack Trainer points out, *'We, as coach educators, must look to give young upcoming coaches the structure and format of how to coach but then allow coaches to coach their own way'*. In other words, it is down to us to create our own unique methods of coaching, something that is far more difficult to do than we may think because we have been influenced by so many (either positively or negatively) already. I can certainly say from personal experience that I have had in-depth discussions with coach educators about particular criticisms of my style of coaching that would not 'fit' the traditional way of coaching and therefore would not pass.

Realistically, we need to focus our structure and content *on the players we have*; this means set ups will change, instructional methods will differ, and goal setting will be individualised in order to meet the demands of *our* players. All of this cannot be met from the current structure promoted on more traditional courses.

Youth Coaching Pathway – the new youth education system in football

With the English game coming under recent scrutiny, the Football Association has had to rethink its strategy – leading to our well-known Youth Modules and Youth Award. The aim is to teach coaches that we no longer need to scream the phrase 'Stop, Stand Still!'. Instead, the Youth Award takes us on an educational journey that encourages coaches to look at the environment, the practice, and the player to foster development.

Having broken the Youth coaching pathway down into three main sections, the youth modules looked far more specifically into what could be done to create better sessions for players. The concept moved from 'what' we were coaching to 'how' we coached. The focus seemingly shifted towards the nature of the interaction with today's youth team players. Importantly, it seemed that the F.A. has recognised the need to take the social aspect of coaching more seriously.

Through the three modules, coach educators are seemingly far more relaxed and informal in their approach to teaching and educating coaches. They offer suggestions and reasons behind creating certain sessions and the bulk of teaching theory is based upon the 'person' and 'player' and how they can be developed (rather than creating a session for a topic). Module 1 *'Developing the Environment'*, was the catalyst for this; one coach educator I know actually commented that much of what would be learned would often contradict the traditional courses and that open-mindedness would be the key.

In module 2, *'Developing the Practice'*, we are given an insight into how we can mould a session around our players, giving far more freedom for coaches and players alike. Finally, in module 3 *'Developing the Player'* we learn that, in order to stretch the player, we must challenge them. Individual, unit, and team goals are the objectives that need to be tried and met in order to progress. On the whole, the youth modules offer something different.

What the Youth Coaching Pathway gives us as coaches to give to players and people

These youth modules, in themselves, are a far cry from the more traditional coaching courses we have been used to in the past. Youth modules offer coaches far more freedom to work with their players and many more options when looking to plan a session.

The biggest change, however, has come from the perception that these youth modules look to develop the player and the person. This is a revelation to see and something that I am excited about being a part of. It gives coaches the idea (certainly at the grassroots level) to work with individuals far more and that it's okay to allow players to make mistakes and to just guide them.

Imagine the benefits of doing this with a player/person in your sessions - taking a player out, asking them questions that start with 'how' rather than 'what'. Looking for answers from the player's own experiences and knowledge rather than giving the answers up. This approach promotes what we need to develop within a person: taking responsibility, problem solving, and interacting with others (coaches and teammates). All of these factors can only be positive when looking to develop our next generation of talent.

So, are there issues with these courses?

Are there issues with the traditional and Youth Module courses? Of course there are! We wouldn't be writing in blogs, on feedback forms, or having discussions with colleagues if there were not. The big issue with these two sets of courses is not necessarily what they do (and do not) offer coaches to give to players. The issue, instead, is the fact that we as coaches have *to do both* in order to see the problem.

Essentially the two sets of courses are at completely opposite ends of the coaching continuum. One gives players limited involvement, based predominantly on the coach and is old fashioned (a 'do as I say' approach). Whereas the other approach gives far more freedom to players, the focus is on the player/person and there is far more variation in teaching methods to integrate into the sessions.

The big issue with the content and delivery of the courses are the mixed messages being translated across the board from different coach educators within the F.A. The unfortunate thing for coaches is that it proves expensive to find out these mixed messages (money, time, travel). Ultimately, it is the players who pay the price because we often revert back to our strongest points as coaches when approached with controversial change.

What looks to be coming and what do we need to create?

There has been a huge ray of shining light recently in the game of football. The 2014 World Cup highlighted one very real and important point… that English football looks set to be changing (finally). The display in England's first game against Italy demonstrated that, when going forward, there were new ideas and the start of a particular style and philosophy of football that everyone seemed to appreciate (regardless of the result).

Every coach could see the benefit of youth, pace, skill and risk in England's frontline and I could just imagine coaches all over the country getting their notepads out and planning sessions around what was being witnessed. One of the main reasons we have found it so hard to create English talent that can play in big international competitions is that the coaches instructing and trying to develop these young players actually have no idea what they are trying to create. It is like an architect trying to design a person's ideal home with no input from the person who wants to live in it. It is effectively impossible to do.

In my opinion, the unfortunate reality is that it really doesn't matter what types of practices or courses the F.A. deliver because ultimately we are missing the most important factor: identity. What I mean by that is that we have no real way of playing, no English style, and ultimately this is because we have no direction. You can distinguish the type of football the likes of Brazil have played in the past, how Barcelona excelled over the past few years, and more recently the successes of Borussia Dortmund and Atletico Madrid. Although this seems to be finally changing, we must hope that this excitement is not restricted to the aftermath of the tournament and it generates the momentum for change.

What we are looking for, from the F.A., is an understanding that in order to develop better youth players, there needs to be a greater understanding of the person as well. The youth modules have begun to do this, however, the message needs to be filtered into more mainstream courses and greater focus placed on the social aspects of development of the player and person. Teaching a player about responsibility, about the need for communication, and giving them the opportunity to solve their problems on the pitch alone and with teammates is an essential part of their development.

Summary

There is more than one way to skin a cat, and there is certainly more than one way to develop a football player.

Coaching courses, both mainstream and youth modules alike, have mimicked the ever-changing educational system, which like football has come under enormous pressure to deliver a wide range of suitable teachings that young players value and which develop knowledge and skills they can use for the rest of their lives. The unfortunate and sad truth of this is that, just like education, football is currently a reactive ecosystem.

Here coaches need to take the time to read and gain knowledge that will suit their players first and foremost, which means developing the player and person. Coaches will have to spend hard-earned time, money and resources on understanding the differences and mixed messages that the F.A. are currently sending out.

The next chapter will now look at the general approaches to coaching and will hopefully give you some ideas to think about, in relation to developing both the person and the player.

4. General Approaches to Coaching

Over the previous chapters, we have looked at many things that football has gone through – some successful, some unsuccessful – and all of which (in my opinion) literally means absolutely nothing, as it should to you. There is almost nothing we, as coaches, can do that ultimately influences what was done in the past, what the F.A. chooses to do now, and what they are likely to do or not do in the future. For all the conferences, suggestion boxes and online surveys, ultimately we have very little (if any) control over football and its development in this country as a whole.

So what are we in charge of?

Looking at things, realistically, we are simply in control of ourselves, and our actions and how we do things that we feel will benefit the players we are responsible for.

We could go on and on, continually criticising the past. How Charles Hughes has negatively affected our country's chances of creating and developing successful homegrown players, how we as a nation fail to implement key concepts that other countries have done so well, or the fact that we are never going to get rid of the issue of football in this country being like a 'boys club'! Instead, what we should be doing is the job we have been hired to do to the best of our abilities. Whether that job is taking a grassroots group of U9's or the Under 18's of a Category 1 Academy side, we are ultimately in charge of our own destiny as coaches.

The most important three areas that I feel we need to work on are: our planning, our session execution, and our ability to reflect with an open mind. These three areas put us in charge of what we do and ultimately make us the coaches we are. They give us the experience necessary to develop and improve ourselves and our players.

Our experiences have often been guided and shaped from what we have seen, and been part of, in the past, some of which can help us in a positive manner; other experiences, however, will feel like the worst kind of experience at the time, but as long as they are reflected upon properly – they can still have a positive effect. I can give a personal example…

At the tender age of 16, I had just got into the coaching game. Coming from a team that I played in where discipline and fitness were essential, I tried to bring that into my own sessions when teaching 10 year olds how to play. I screamed, I shouted, they got worse and eventually I got another coach to take over. I remember sitting on the grass after the session asking myself why they weren't improving and why they trained so poorly. I questioned the players' abilities and told myself they weren't good enough. I mean I had played for a team that - through discipline and fitness - had won a league and cup double the previous season, so it must have been the players! I look back at that session now with a smile on my face and the thought of 'what a terrible job you did there Noel'.

I look back at that session and many more like it in my early coaching days and recognise and understand that it was my approach to coaching the session that affected the players. I learned that there was nothing wrong with my underlying values (respect, discipline and effort) but I portrayed them in such a regimented way that I created a fear of failure within the sessions. This was huge for me; my approach had to change which meant my planning had to change, taking out drills and putting in games. My challenges had to change for the group, my expectations were as high as ever but I asked myself the question as if I was a player playing in my sessions, 'If I got something wrong in training, how would I want my coach to react with me?'

Factors to consider

There are a number of different approaches and styles of coaching that have been identified and discussed in recent years. Some approaches come from the world of sport, others from academia, many are useful and insightful; however, what must be understood is that only *you* can decide how *you* want to coach. Coach educators can explain and demonstrate what could be done with groups but ultimately it is down to you whether you take on a particular style or approach.

When deciding what approach(es) to take there are a number of factors that must be considered:

Age of Players	Ability levels	Environment	Facilities
Location of team	Learner types	Equipment	Reason for playing
Length of Session	Behavioural factors	Social factors	Expectations from club
Your philosophy	Your understanding of the game	Type of session	Expectations of parents/fans

The above factors are just a few that need to be considered when you are planning a coaching session and yet most of us think about the majority of them without too much effort. I believe it is the attention to this kind of detail that makes a huge difference to sessions and ultimately the development of our players.

Approaches/Styles to consider

Autocratic/ Command Style Approach

The autocratic approach to coaching is an interesting one, especially in modern day football coaching. This approach defines itself as being a coach-orientated 'telling' approach, where instructions are given by the coach about what they want to achieve in a particular session or drill. The players then execute those instructions to the best of their abilities. There is minimal input from players under this approach.

This approach is somewhat militarized, where players are seen as the soldiers and the coach as the General. This approach often creates an environment of good discipline, respect for authority, and good levels of organisation in training and in games. There are, however, a number of issues with this style. In today's game footballers appear to have greater influence and power due to the nature of the sport. The industry is seen far more as a business with managing directors, agents and endorsements, and the players at the top level can often find themselves giving their opinions to managers and coaches far more. The autocratic approach has little room for that.

Here the coach's word is final; it's the coach's decisions that rule and often you will find players' morale affected if they do not agree with a coach's decision. Accordingly, the delivery of top class performances does not occur consistently. At the professional level, this approach certainly suffers more now due to technological advances and the vast media coverage available to us all. Any kind of disruption in a team or clash of personalities is pounced on by the whole country and subsequent rumours surrounding the coach can snowball within a matter of hours.

Despite the issues highlighted, some of the best coaches in the world have taken up this approach to coaching. Looking at the likes of Sir Alex Ferguson, Jose Mourinho and Brain Clough - they all dictated what they wanted to see from their teams and it was their way or the highway (so to speak).

Democratic/ Reciprocal Style Approach

The democratic approach to coaching is a far more cooperative style when compared to the autocratic approach. Here, coaches and players can share a range of ideas and players have heightened participation in the decision-making processes underlying training sessions. The coach will still be in charge and will ultimately make the final decision on areas such as objectives and goals for the session but players and the coach will discuss ways to achieve those goals and objectives.

This approach to coaching can give players a sense of accountability and self-control over their learning. Here players often have choices that will allow the group to help shape the training session towards particular goals set out by the coach. In turn, players often feel as though they have the freedom to express themselves through chosen activities, and coaches should allow for this freedom when coaching and giving instructions.

By giving players this sense of control over the session, you are not just developing their football skills but also enhancing other important skills such as communication, organisation, and problem solving, all of which are *essential* when looking to develop players individually and as a unit and team. Coaches should expect to see some excellent development all round, as a player and as a person, in relation to social skills.

Coaches must be careful, however, not to allow players to rule the entire session. Depending on the level of player, and understanding of the game, players may actually struggle to put a session on that they feel could help them and will often just put a session on that suits them. Also, not all players may agree on what the best type of session is - which may lead to conflict and the more socially dominant players putting on the sessions that they want. Even with coach intervention, some players may still feel that their points are not considered, and subsequently become demotivated.

Once again, there are pros and cons to this approach and if managed well by the coach the democratic approach can often lead to some excellent sessions taking place; sessions filled with ownership, empowerment, and responsibility.

Laissez-Faire /Guided Discovery Style Approach

The approach known as the laissez-faire approach (loosely translated to mean 'letting people do as they please') is another option for the coach. Here players are given complete freedom to a session, and are in charge of the entire session, including the aims, type of session, and content. Here, coaches take a major step back and observe the players. It promotes problem solving skills and decision making from players and encourages (and potentially develops) social skills amongst the group.

This approach has attracted a lot of criticism across a range of sectors (business, leadership, education) as its method of leaving people to their own devices often leads to low motivation as clear goals are often not set. A player's work ethic can also decrease as there is no leader to govern the session and this can subsequently impact on team morale and group motivation.

Many coaches have chosen to steer clear of this approach but there can be some huge positive impacts here. Like any other situation, applying this approach to a more elite group of players who are highly skilled and intelligent can be very advantageous. Allowing the right players the freedom to express themselves can often lead to greater performance and development, which at times can have a positive effect on the rest of the group.

By guiding players and giving them feedback such as verbal instruction, practical demonstration, or visual aids (whiteboards, iPads) you are allowing them to not only develop techniques and tactics within the game but you are also giving them the potential to make themselves a better and more developed person: learning and understanding how their own behaviours impact upon their own performance and others around them. It will also help enhance responsibility, the need for effective organisation, and time management.

Holistic/Whole Person Approach

This final approach is often seen as the 'whole' person approach. Its roots stem from more of a lifestyle coaching perspective and it makes use of neuro linguistic programming (NLP) to improve people's lives in mainstream society. This approach involves looking at what constitutes a person as a whole and breaks down that individual. Here factors such as society, education, mentality, physicality, and personality are all looked at (as each has their own effect on the whole person). In essence, the holistic approach states that everything we do has a particular cause or a reason behind it and will end in a particular effect, whether it is a desired one or not.

It is here that sport can learn a lot; this holistic approach has not gained much attention as clubs, and nations are often not too bothered about the player as a person. This is why we have typically seen the other three approaches take precedence. However, it now seems to be becoming clearer that in order to develop the modern day player who can cope at the top level, we must look beyond standard practice and training approaches.

With greater demands to develop youth players who are good enough to play in academies, and who develop through to the professional game, we must prepare the players for more than just footballing demands, and look at issues that may occur away from the training ground. We must delve a lot deeper into the person.

This approach looks to take on-board other areas and issues such as mental and social wellbeing and understanding - in order to help develop players technically, tactically and physically on the training field and in games. This approach concerns itself with understanding actions in relation to the whole world, and aims to give players a greater understanding and sense of purpose in their life. It can help to develop a satisfaction within people to feel calmer, happier and more content with their contributions.

It hasn't been until recently that sport has taken on this more holistic approach, Terry Orlick, a Professor in Human Kinetics, along with Andrew Friesen wrote a journal article, in 2011, on what sport psychologists were doing to create far more holistic interventions for athletes in sport and what consultants are now doing to aid the athletes they come into contact with. Sports Coach UK have also created their own ten-minute video entitled *'Coaching the Whole Child',* which comments on the importance of building children's self-esteem and confidence through a far more holistic approach. One basketball coach from the video states that: *We as coaches have a responsibility to develop the whole person, and we use sport as a kind of medium to help develop other skills'*. It was commented that this approach can help children with lifestyle choices to better their future prospects. It also has them thinking about their behaviours.

This approach takes many things on-board and a lot into consideration, which at times is one of its potential problems. It can be seen as a very time consuming approach, especially if you are dealing with a large squad of players that you only see once a week (which is often the case within grassroots football). Another issue is that you, as the coach, may at times be interfering in aspects of a child's life that do not concern you. In turn, you may not always be able to put across the very broad outlook of the holistic approach and make it applicable to sport or football in the ways you want.

Summary of Approaches

From looking at the different approaches to coaching, above, we can all agree that at some stage we have been part of, in charge of, or been led by a particular approach. What must be stressed, especially in the UK, is that the wonderful world of professional football and coaching is available to very few on a full time basis and more often than not coaches are expected to juggle their regular day-to-day jobs while still trying to plan effective coaching sessions.

The benefit of understanding these basic approaches to coaching is that they should govern the type of session you create and the content within it. Coaches need to think about how we want to engage with our players and how best we can go about doing that. Of course, not all approaches will work with everyone and each person should be getting an individualised approach whenever possible. However, your approach should mimic your own philosophy of coaching that will allow you to plan your sessions effectively. Here follows a table with the pros and cons of typical coaching approaches.

Style	Pros	Cons
Autocratic	*Increased levels of:* Respect Discipline Organisation	Coach orientated Limited player input Can result in decreased motivation levels in players
Democratic	*More:* Accountability Responsibility Communication between players and coaches	Can be time consuming if agreements cannot be made Can affect players who feel they are not being listened to
Laissez Faire	*Greater:* Ownership Freedom	Players become demotivated Work ethic decreases
Holistic	*Development of a:* Greater understanding of self Sense of accomplishment	Not easily applicable to sport Very time consuming Could interfere in aspects of life that do not concern you

What will benefit the player and person the most?

The above approaches have all been tried and tested in a range of different industries (business, leadership, child development) and each have their own strengths and weaknesses; for the coach it is not really about picking one over the other.

There is certainly a need for coaches of the modern game to flutter between all coaching approaches throughout the season and it is even more important for a coach to understand *why* this needs be the case. A colleague of mine who is also a teacher and an academy coach at a Premier League club discussed the analogy of 'Soldiers vs. Artists'; (he commented that our approaches should be very individual to the player and person and that you should get to know your players before deciding on a particular approach.)

He stated that 'soldiers', who develop from an early age, need clear rules and boundaries to be set for them and an autocratic approach used when you are looking for particular techniques to be carried out correctly (for example dribbling technique or passing). Here you are looking to instil a set of fundamentals, which can still be done in a fun game-type session. The reason for this is that all youth players, at some stage, will observe what others are doing and follow that person. Here, the coach can be the centre of attention (for a short period) and demonstrate, instruct, and guide exactly what he wants players to try to do. For personal development, you are also introducing and instilling values such as respect, discipline, and responsibility.

'Artists' however need a different approach. These types of players are associated with being very creative and have a high level of game intelligence – so you would take a far more laissez faire or democratic approach. The focus would be to allow this player to make their own decisions and the coach's role would simply be to guide and facilitate, and point them in the right direction. Again, you are still able to work with the person just as much as the player, ensuring life skills such as taking responsibility for one's actions are developed and understood - making both player and person more independent.

The interesting point here, with all the approaches, is that no one method should be thought of as age-specific. Yes, one particular approach may work better at a younger or older age but the important thing is to get to know your players: speak to them and find out what makes them tick. Coaches need to go beyond the traditional football talk on the training pitch. They need to take time out to stay after training or games, speak with parents and friends of the players. Coaches need to really engage that person in every session.

You also have to consider ability and participation when deciding on your approach; you could easily take up a far more laissez faire approach with an U10 academy side, whereas an U16 grassroots team may need a very strict autocratic approach. I can certainly recall, from previous experiences, the need to set basic rules and boundaries for an U18 team, players whom I thought would be responsible for themselves and others. When employed by a League One academy club and coaching the U13 squad it was amazing to see that I didn't once have to bring up basic rules for players to adhere to… the autocratic approach was never needed.

Summary

Whatever approach you are looking to use, whether it is one of the four described above or any others, it is not important which one you use but your understanding of *why* you are using it. Approaches should be geared towards your football philosophy but coaches must be open-minded and get to know their players in order to man-manage them with different approaches in training and in games. This means getting to know the person and not just looking at the player on the pitch, deciding whether they are a soldier or an artist (or something else) and interacting with and coaching them accordingly.

5. Methods of teaching, training and coaching

Profound responsibilities come with teaching and coaching. You can do so much good – or harm. It's why I believe that next to parenting, teaching and coaching are the two most important professions in the world. John Wooden

The above quote came from a man that I knew little about and from a book that completely turned my teaching and coaching world upside down. John Wooden was an American College basketball coach and English teacher who broke almost every record going in college basketball in the U.S. The All-American, Hall of fame player and coach, left a lasting legacy at the University of California Los Angeles (UCLA) and gave me the inspiration to write this particular chapter.

In this chapter, I hope to offer what Coach Wooden did for me in a way that aids the development of players and people alike. There is, of course, a large literature out there, which you may have already seen and appreciated (even discarded). However, I challenge you to keep an open mind about the questions asked of us as coaches and teachers and how they could impact on the player and the person.

'What' are we trying to coach?

A seemingly basic and apparently easy question to answer at first glance; the answer is generally along the lines of 'we are coaching players to become better at football' and that answer would, of course, be correct. Fundamentally, that is what we are here for! However, if we want to get the most out of our players, and ourselves, we must dig a lot deeper. What are we really trying to do?

Well, looking at coaching from the beginning and what is required is often known as 'the basics' or 'fundamentals' of football. These fundamentals have been broken up into what is commonly known as the '4 corner model'.

The table below illustrates some of the basic fundamentals that I feel all players should be coached on from a young age. Obviously, some of these will differ in importance and coaches may add or delete some elements. Whatever the case, we must understand exactly 'what' we need to be teaching in order for us to effectively teach so that the players can learn. The following table lists some of the fundamentals needed to play.

Technical	Tactical	Social/ Psychological	Physical
Dribbling Control Turning Passing Shooting Heading Tackling Running with the ball	Positional sense (within a number of different positions) Awareness (of self and others) Understanding of basic formations Learn systems/styles of play	Communication Cohesion Understanding and accepting roles Building confidence Developing concentration to detail Improving decision making	Not overly focused on physicality as: Sessions can be physically demanding anyway if prepared properly Higher level players should be doing their own fitness Clubs have specialist departments to complete this component

When looking at Table 1, I wonder whether I actually hit all of those fundamentals during my sessions. Many coaches, managers and educators will argue that 'we do all of that without really thinking' but that is not acceptable when looking to develop your players. 'What' you coach must be broken down and taught effectively if you want your players to learn.

Some of the most successful teams in world sport have based their success around fundamentals. The famous Tennessee Titans, a high school American football team, saw their claim to fame come from their autocratic coach Herman Boone's strict coaching of fundamentals. His thin playbook was irrelevant because the team succeeded in doing the basics well.

More recently, in 2014, San Antonio Spurs basketball team were crowned NBA champions and their success was put down to their fluid passing game, rigid defensive unit, and team cohesion – fundamentals in basketball.

John Wooden's very own UCLA legacy – 10 national titles in 12 years (including 7 in a row) – was based around the fundamentals of discipline, reliability and doing the basic technical and tactical skills well. In football, Chelsea's 2004-05 Premier League title-winning side was victorious thanks to the fundamentals of a solid defensive unit and players understanding their roles within the squad. More recently, we have seen the success of the German national side and German clubs due to strict player roles within the team, high levels of fitness, and acute efficiency on the counter attack.

When you break down winning sides, they do not necessarily do 7-10 things right, often they stick to a few essential principles of play and do these extremely well.

What we are ultimately trying to develop within our players is automaticity, that is, players carrying out a set of actions without having to think about them. We want actions to become second nature. It is my belief that too many of us (including myself at times) forget about this and try to teach players too much too soon. I have found myself, on a number of occasions, thinking and planning out a seemingly complex session with a title such as 'overlapping runs from the full back to create width in order to cross to the central striker' before realising I am wasting my time and my players' time. Why? Because they can't do the basics!

Nowadays, I take it as my responsibility, first and foremost, to have my players perform all the fundamentals in that table until they become second nature.

I would stress to coaches at grassroots, academy and professional level to develop their players to excel in the basics and to do so consistently. Even in the modern game – in this country – there are too many players who are overly dependent on one side (foot, thigh, vision). Academies, the Premier League, and the Football League develop curricula in great detail to achieve EPPP status (with fancy session titles and diagrams and coaching points) and sometimes fall short in seeing what is truly required!

'Why' are we coaching?

There are many reasons why we coach football: passion, providing for our families, helping others out. Whatever the reasoning behind 'why' you coach football, it is important to understand that everything you do should be for the benefit of the player and person. This approach has been termed the 'player centred approach' and, as the name suggests, it makes players the centre of attention. Its aim is to ensure that the sessions you put on, and the advice and help you give players, should be to make them better players.

It is extremely important for a coach to sit down and really think about what they do and why they do it. Many coaches get into coaching for the wrong reasons and are often found out because of it.

Many coaches will understand just how important their contribution to a child's development really is, echoing the quote at the start of the chapter. Coaches have the potential to do so much good, but also have the ability to harm a child's development as a person as well as a player. Coaches must also understand that much of what they do will go unnoticed and will often receive little recognition. It means that coaches must be intrinsically motivated to improve and develop a child.

Coaches must look to nurture, guide and facilitate players and people into making their own decisions, making them responsible for their own development and ensuring that – if they do trip and fall (which all players will almost certainly do at some stage) – they are there to pick them back up with a caring and enthusiastic approach (and some knowledgeable advice the player can take on board). I would encourage all coaches, before deciding on the type of session and what drill to use, to decide 'what you are coaching, and 'why' you are coaching it. Let the answers then shape what you create from there.

Types of Practices Used to Coach

The above areas, the 'what, why, how', should be at the forefront of every coach's mind when looking to develop their players as footballers and as individuals. It must be made clear that this cannot be the case in every session due to a number of constraints (time, facilities, equipment, ability levels, and age).

Below are descriptions of a range of different types of sessions that coaches can put together. There are, of course, almost an unlimited supply of sessions available to us in this day and age, but for the purpose of simplicity (and my own sanity of writing) I have chosen to describe seven main types of practice that I feel will benefit players the most.

1. Games orientated programme/teaching games for Understanding (TGfU)

The first type of practice is what I see as a games-orientated approach, known better as teaching games for understanding (TGfU). This approach, developed in the early 1980's has received a lot of academic attention. Researchers believe that this form of coaching/training should be taking the lead in sessions across a range of sports. Hopper and Kruisselbrink (2002) described TGfU as something that "...*focuses upon teaching students tactical understanding before dealing with the performance of skills, as such the TGfU offers a tactical approach to games teaching emphasizing game performance before skill performance.*"

TGfU aims to teach the person or player tactical elements of the game, including rules and regulations, in a way that is conducive to the sport itself. Within that, a coach can embed the techniques and skills associated with that sport. The creation of TGfU is often broken down into phases, and the following is a basic illustration of what could be included and what can be built into sessions as players progress.

1. Creating four games linked to passing and receiving: Focus can be placed on: Short passes Long passes Overhead passes Wrap passes	2. Games relate to the normal rules and regulations of football and are adhered to at all times. Allow players to grasp the rules, patterns, tactics and techniques within the game Here formations can be set out to mimic game-like situations
3. The coach embeds some technical information to aid in passing and receiving the ball: How to receive Surface of boot Passing technique	4. The coach can then work on more social and mental aspects, bringing in areas such as: Communication Organisation

One of the biggest issues with the TGfU approach is that it somewhat devalues the need for players to be able to demonstrate, and carry out, basic skills and techniques associated with football (this could be as simple as controlling a ball). If players are unable to perform this skill then too much time will be wasted in games retrieving footballs and the flow of the game will cease to exist. Accordingly, there will be few game understanding opportunities for players. This is likely to occur with younger age groups, or lower ability groups, so must be managed accordingly.

You may wish to use the TGfU method with slightly older or higher ability groups that have already mastered the basic technical skills needed to effectively play the game. This allows for a greater tactical understanding and application of rules and regulations which can have a greater effect on players. The following illustration shows the potential of what can be achieved using this method of training.

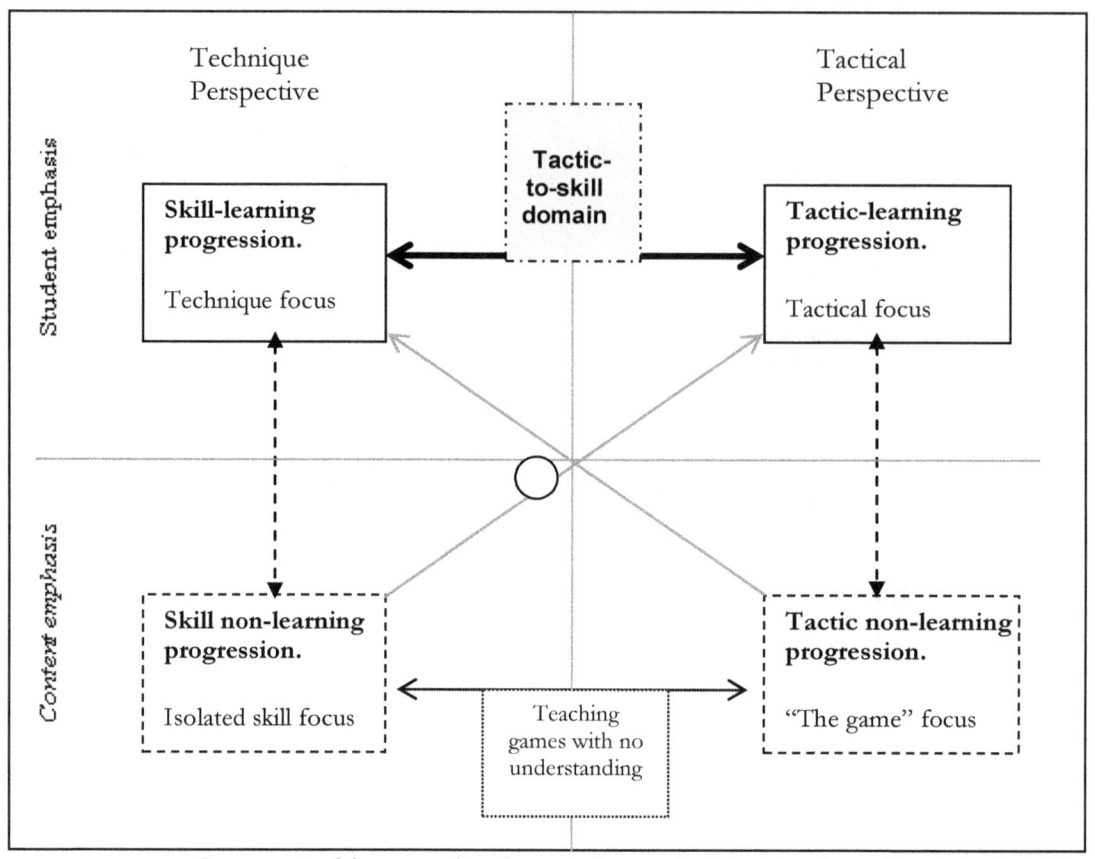

Games teaching matrix: Comparing techniques and tactics

The nature of this 'game focus' is to provide and develop 'in game' understanding of situations that are likely to occur from the very start of the session. This, in turn, aids in the development of match-related skills, techniques, and awareness.

2. Whole-Part Practice

Another type of practice that gained prominence with the creation of Youth Modules was Whole-Part practice. It is not a new concept, though, having been used as early as the 1930's in Basketball, American Football, and more recently in Rugby.

Football has taken this method of training on-board due to the freedom it gives players to express themselves in a game-like situation for two thirds of a session. Coaches are still able to give detailed technical/tactical coaching for the other third. Sessions are divided into three main parts:

Whole	Coaches create a game-like situation or open practice with a pre-planned objective; players are given the freedom to play under the understanding that the coach is looking for a particular objective to be met.
Part	Once the whole practice has been established, coaches are then able to focus on smaller 'parts' to build on player ability and understanding. This is often demonstrated in the form of a smaller numbered practice that involves specific elements of the topic being delivered.
Whole	Players are then put back into the 'whole' or game where newly developed skills are given the chance to flourish; here coaches are looking for what has been taught. Stoppages should be minimal and adjustments to individual play should be done by taking a player out quickly, explaining key points, and putting them straight back in.

The idea of allowing players to try to achieve an objective even before it has been broken down can give the player and person great satisfaction and increase levels of confidence and motivation. This may then spur others on to achieve, and can often have positive effects on training intensity and group cohesion.

Below are two examples of how the whole-part method of training can be brought into your sessions. Coaches will generally use this with an individual player looking at a particular skill/technique to improve on their own, or will deliver a session based on developing a unit or whole team's style of play.

Example of using Whole-Part Practice for an individual technical development practice:

	Session Title: Developing a player's ability to dribble the ball
Whole	The coach has an individual player dribbling around a specified area (box 10x10/20x20). The coach observes dribbling technique and gives short instructions as to what they are looking to see. The player should be dribbling at all times and not stopping the ball from moving.
Part	The coach may then stop the practice and break down each element of what they want to see. Demonstration and technical instruction may be given to guide the player into how they can dribble the ball: (Inside Outside/Big Toe Little Toe) *Cushion the ball with the inside of your boot, level with your big toe, changing the angle and direction of the ball.* *Bring your boot around the ball and touch the ball with the outside of your boot, level with your little toe - to affect the angle and direction of the ball.* *Adjust your body shape to come inside of the ball and around the ball.* *Head up, looking ahead* *Arms out for balance*
Whole	Allows players to dribble the ball at normal speed again. Can incorporate additional challenges to make dribbling more difficult (incorporate roll, step over, and change of direction every four touches).

This type of Whole-Part practice isolates a particular technique and should be carried out in small doses (we will discuss this in more detail with the next method).

It can often aid players who are young, or of a lesser ability, to pick up the basics by giving them a few key teaching points along with demonstration and guidance.

Example of using Whole-Part in a unit/team session:

Session Title: Combination play to get behind a defensive unit	
Whole	The coach will set up a 6v6/8v8, for example, with the session title put up on a whiteboard. The coach explains the objective of the session and encourages both teams to make use of combination play. The coach may ask players what they think combination play means and allow players to answer. The coach then gives players the freedom to go and play, while trying to meet the session objective.
Part	The coach will then have a smaller 'part' practice set up that works specifically on 2-3 passing combinations that they wish to see from their players. These combinations may be practiced with no opposition at first (pattern), followed by an attacking overload at half speed, and then full speed (3v1/4v2). Coaches my also wish to break down each pass and movement off the ball ($2^{nd}/3^{rd}$ player runs, first time cushion pass/wrap pass).
Whole	Players are put back into the 6v6/8v8 game situation. Players are again given the freedom to play how they wish. The coach is now looking for the combinations worked on in the part phase. Stoppages are minimal, allowing for free play to occur once again.

Coaches must ensure that this method of training is used at the right times and with the right players. I have seen many coaches attend the Youth Module 2 course where developing practice is the focus (with this Whole-Part method as its primary method) and they come out with the feeling that this is the 'only' method to use.

Coaches must ensure that the 'part' practices are not boring as players will often switch off and become more concerned with getting back to the game situation. If the part practice is dull, they will not take on-board the breakdown of what is required.

3. Isolation training (in small doses)

This has been a hotly debated area of training within football for the last few years, with many coaches questioning the use of isolation training altogether. Like any other form of training there are pros and cons, and many argue that the major drawback of isolation training is that it does not mimic any form of the game and takes away game understanding which is deemed essential for developing elite football players.

The issue certainly has merit as there is no doubt that top players have an in-depth understanding of the game. My only issue, however, is that - do players aged 5-12 years old really need to have all of this game understanding at such an early age?

I have seen so many sessions carried out that look at inclusive practice – 'techniques being developed within skill-based games' – and it all sounds amazing! Yet watching the majority of these, practices and games break down after two passes - because players have not yet learnt to control the ball - is baffling. It's like asking a baby to run before it has even stood up! I see great value in isolation-based drills due to the specific nature of focusing on just one thing, but I always use the analogy of learning to read: 'you must learn each individual word first before you can understand the meaning of a sentence' and I feel the same is true of football techniques: if you cannot dribble, how will you ever get into a position where you have to make a decision on when, where, and how to dribble the ball?

I am not saying that coaches should be spending hours on isolation drills but spending 5-10 minutes a session on a different range of techniques does (I feel) far more good than harm, especially with younger age groups. Each player will be different and excel at different technical elements, which can give the coach time to focus on one particular technical skill they'd like the player to progress with. This gives players a chance to show off their techniques in a 10-minute spell and can also instil confidence and challenge players to try new things without the fear of initially being tackled. They can focus their energy on getting things right. I have never seen a player do a step over in a skilled practice/game situation, which had not been developed in isolation.

We need to understand what players already know (questioning players can gauge this quickly) and understand that development doesn't need to come all at once. If you take a look at Germany and Belgium, for example, they do not get players involved in intense training until the age of 14, yet their national youth teams and full national sides appear to understand the game pretty well! So consider the importance of isolation but, as the title suggests, use it in small doses.

4. Small sided games

Small sided games or SSG's are a fantastic way to build players' techniques into skills and develop game understanding through a wide variety of short, sharp, and intense games. Here coaches, like players need to know where, when, and how, to use SSG's. Putting a game into the end of a practice has often been seen as the norm in this country; however, more recently (with the introduction of Youth Modules and whole-part-whole practice) games are often used to start a session.

Each SSG must have a specific aim; accordingly, this should be in line with the whole aim of the session and coaching plan. Although often seen as a 'get out' by many coaches (letting players play a game often means coaches switch off and take a step back) SSG's must be carefully structured and challenges, rules, boundaries given - if you want the aim of your session to be met. Although, at times, having the coach stand back and observe things can be beneficial, it is more important for the coach to be vigilant and pick out elements of team and individual play that can be worked on. Often coaches can identify the material for (potentially) another four weeks' worth of sessions after watching SSG's as they highlight a number of game-orientated issues that need work.

SSG's are also the perfect way to work with individual players on a more personal level as you can be more concerned with the execution of moves (patterns of play). This not only involves techniques and football skills but other skills such as communication, organisation, confidence and adaptability. All of these areas you will need to coach so that they are geared towards the individual. You may pull a player aside or you may stop the whole practice in order to effectively provide instruction. Your own communication here will affect how players react, and is one of the reasons that SSG's must be planned before execution so you understand the types of pictures/scenarios that will most likely come from the session.

Other types of Practice

1. Functions

Functions of play focus on a specific position or area of the pitch. Often carried out to focus on one player or a unit (e.g. centre back pair). Generally associated with more of the core coaching pathway, functions are a great method to use if you want to work with a particular unit or group of players in a particular area of the pitch.

Functions help maintain game realism (due to position-specific work) and allow you to break elements of your session down to help improve game understanding.

2. Phases of Play (PoP)

Phases of play are larger types of practice (often covering two thirds of a pitch) that focus on whole units or an entire team in particular patterns of play or tactical understanding within a specific formation for example. These are almost an 'add on' from functions. Coaches are able to work with larger numbers of players to help them see pictures and patterns that are most likely to occur during actual game play. This type of practice gives players a more game-related feel (as long as play is allowed to continue and is not stopped too often). Here coaches are able to work with individuals, pairs, units, or the whole team - developing patterns of play, understanding roles and responsibilities in a particular formation, or improving the organisation of team shape in both attacking and defensive phases of the game.

3. Wave

Wave practices often involve a two-way directional practice involving three or more teams on a particular topic (counter attacking) that allows for quick transitions between phases within the practice. This type of practice has resurfaced into both youth modules and the new format of the UEFA B coaching license. This type of practice is good for getting players used to a particular pattern of play, for example how to counter attack when you have the overload, or the opposite (defending the counter attack when outnumbered). Waves allow for short sharp and precise patterns of play to be developed and can give a lot of freedom to the more creative players in a squad.

Methods of coaching

As well as the different types of practice available to coaches, it is probably even more important to decide how we interact and coach particular topics in our sessions. Here, it is essential to know not just the player but the person as well. Most coaches need to spend a lot more time observing and watching how their own players learn.

It can be very difficult for coaches to see what their players require. Having an hour a week with a player is often not enough time to get to grips with requirements, so it may be the case that we put on a range of different sessions throughout pre-season, for example, to gauge the types of sessions players respond to. Another simple and effective thing to do is to ask players what they require. Allow for openness and honesty from them in what they are looking for. Coaches can then decide how best to plan and execute their sessions to benefit player and person.

Below are a range of methods that can be used to develop both the person and the player on the training pitch and in games. Again, many coaches will already know these methods inside out but I would encourage you to think about how you use these methods and whether you are using them to develop the player only. How else could these methods be used to further develop our young players?

1. Guided discovery

Guided discovery is a method that allows coaches to put forward a particular problem and then allows the players to find suitable solutions within the game. For the modern day coach guided discovery is one approach that we all have to take on-board. The modern player needs time to develop, and needs to be given plenty of opportunity to work on the skills required to become a professional footballer.

Although a fantastic method to use within sessions, it does come with a huge warning sticker attached to it! Guided discovery must be incorporated into the session during the planning stages. Many coaches, including myself in the past, have used guided discovery on a whim. Many coaches fall into the habit of assuming that because the game doesn't change, the rules don't change, and the aim is ultimately the same (to score a goal) that we can leave the players to their own devices and they will continue to work things out for themselves.

However, what is key about guided discovery is that the player recognises the difference between what they are trying to achieve in every session (which is dependent on the topic) and make a correlation to what is likely to happen within a game. They should look to discover outcomes for particular scenarios within the game that vary for different reasons (a player sent off early, conceding a late goal, the main forward going off with an injury). Here, coaching is essential to give the players the scenario and indicate what you are looking for; after all there is no point in just leaving the players to it completely. They will still need guidance, still need a clue or a suggestion, every now and then.

What this method allows for is plenty of game-related repetition, and trial and error. Coaches must expect and encourage failure as long as new things are being tried throughout any session by the players. Coaches' work should come in the form of observation and 'pick and choose' moments to go in and coach (rather than stopping the session every few minutes). Within a session guided discovery must be game-related at all times, often working with particular individuals in key roles (the number 10 or the 4), or working with particular units within phases of the game (defence during a loss in possession in the middle third).

2. Demonstration

Another powerful method to aid development with youth players is using demonstration to 'show' our players what we are looking for. Presented to many coaches in the more traditional courses laid on by the F.A. demonstration gave us a means to show and instruct our players what we wanted to see.

The use of demonstration in the past few years, however, has become something that many coaches now fear. With the introduction of youth modules coaches steered away from the massed use of demonstration because it took away players' 'playing time'. Some coaches stopped giving practical demonstrations as they felt it took away creative freedom from players.

Now coaches use demonstration for more technical elements of coaching. They will show players a particular dribbling technique, a turn, or a step over. Other than for techniques, coaches now often steer clear of giving practical demonstration and instead give players time and opportunity to work out things for themselves.

However effective this is, though, I am not so sure. Of course I am not saying we all have stopped giving demonstrations, however I have seen a rapid decline in the number of demonstrations given during training sessions over the past few seasons and for the life of me I cannot work out why. As coaches we want our players to play in a certain way, as long as our philosophies are player- centred, and promote the right type of football (whatever that may mean to you) then taking time out to demonstrate and replicate the styles of play you want in phases, functions and SSG's should be just as much a part of your coaching than any other.

Coaches may not always provide demonstrations themselves; coaches often use other players, or show short video clips of what they wish to see from their players. This can often be just as effective if you have the resources. Coaches should value the art of demonstration, especially with younger age groups; although we want to give our players the freedom to express themselves and learn they will always need a helping hand so why not show them how to start?

3. Technical instruction

Another extremely important method of coaching is that of technical instruction. This is often accompanied by demonstration, as we want our young players to gain knowledge and understanding of what they are doing. Coaches will spend a lot of time (especially in the Foundation Phase) giving technical information to players.

We spend this time trying to develop individual player's technical ability; their dribbling, turning, receiving, and passing all require technical pointers. But how much information is needed? Having watched experienced coaches give technical instruction across a range of different skills, it was a massive eye opener and I question sometimes, just how much players need to know. I feel younger age groups will need technical instruction communicated at their level, for example, coaches cannot use terminology that includes commenting on ankle, knee, and hip alignment when working on approaches to (and striking) the ball. Instead, coaches may simply say to players how important it is to approach the ball straight on, when possible, and make sure their leg is in a nice straight line. As players get older coaches should use terminology that is more advanced as you want players to learn terminology as well as technical skills.

When coaching a player in defending 1v1 here are some of the technical points that may be considered and used:

1. Get out to the player quickly
2. Slow down before you approach your opponent to prevent the attacker knocking the ball past you with one touch
3. Sit yourself down low
4. Show the attacking player onto his weaker side (whether that is foot, or the opposing team's philosophy of showing on the outside or inside)
5. Slide your feet when you move, do not cross over
6. Arms out slightly for balance (and can often point the attacker to where you want them to go)
7. Eyes fixed on the ball, do not watch the attacker's feet

These seven points are often given before a player has even gone in for a challenge with an opposition player and shows the vast amount of information players need to take on-board in order to progress. Couple this with training often being attended after a full day of school and you begin to see the issues with why players may not take on everything a coach says. As important as technical information is, what coaches must understand is that we can often overload players. This leads to a decline in performance, which then affects motivation, confidence, and a negative snowballing effect ensues.

What I have found is 'planning is everything' here. Although we look to provide continuous technical information in every session (often in small doses), coaches need to plan when technical information is going to be given en masse. You may choose to couple technical instruction with isolation training within every session or few sessions. We all know why technical information is used and needed but we must look to question how often we use it, when and where it is needed, and whether we are overloading players.

4. Challenges

Introduced a lot more in youth modules (specifically module 3), 'challenges' is a method used by a lot of coaches to try to push players to achieve a particular goal(s) within a session. Here coaches are able to hand out team, unit, and individual challenges within almost every session.

Often coaches will hand out challenges that begin with the words 'try to':

Score with a 1 touch finish
Retain the ball after winning a tackle or interception
Decide when it is best to pass to feet or pass to space
Play 1-2 touch football when it is on to do so
Use wide areas of the pitch to set up attacks in the middle

Here, we want players to attempt particular challenges linked to the philosophy we have instilled in the club/team. This is because clubs want players to play in a particular way based on their position, style of team play, or how it links to the first team.

As always, there are some caveats with challenges. Firstly, it is essential that you do not overload any player with challenges; considering that you may be giving them technical and tactics instructions as well, the last thing you want to do is give them yet more things to think about. Secondly, when giving out challenges, it is not as simple as telling a player what you want them to do. Challenges need to be monitored and observed to the extent that players are able to recognise when they are achieving them. For example, unless you are able to record pass success (tally charts), there is no point in asking a midfielder to complete 90% of their passes to teammates.

5. Questioning

Questioning, since the introduction of the Youth award, has stepped back into the limelight. Questioning, in itself, is a method of obtaining information to clarify a point or to test knowledge and coaches are now using it to gauge where their squad is (in terms of game understanding, individual roles on the pitch, and knowing what is expected of players).

Questioning can be a powerful tool in the development of talent, however questioning can become an issue at times. Firstly, the art of questioning is knowing not always *what* question to ask but *when* and *how* to ask it. I have seen coaches using questioning (I have done this myself) so often in sessions that players quickly learn what might be termed 'textbook' answers. The players tell the coach what they want to hear.

Players will answer direct or indirect questions perfectly when in a huddle, or when taking a break but how many coaches ask a question such as: *'How do we stop the opposition having time and space in the middle of the pitch?'* and the players answer with *'close the space quickly, hunt in packs, pick up the man closet to you'*. Initially you think – great, they've got it! – yet not two minutes will pass and the opposition will have time and space in the middle of the park.

What coaches must consider is, are they asking the right questions at the right times? Is it specific to the development of the individual? Many of us (certainly including me at times) forget that although it is a team game we must first develop the individual player. Teaching skills and techniques is one thing, but helping players to understand 'why' they are doing something is even more important.

One exercise I developed was called 'the 5 minute why/why not game' (not very imaginative I know!). I set up a normal game (SSG 4v4/5v5/6v6) and explained to the players what I would be doing. For the first minute they would have free play, then with stopwatch in hand I would spend the next three minutes stopping the game every few passes/phases and ask players on, around, and away from the ball 'why'. Why did a particular player make that pass and not another? Why was a player stood still? Why did that player move there and not there? Why didn't you shoot? Everything was why. I wanted to gain an understanding of what my players were doing in their heads to make the decisions they were making (good and bad decisions) and I wanted them to think about it too. The last minute was then spent with free play.

It is a method I use every now and then, as stopping a game can be quite frustrating. The exercise paid dividends over the course of the season as player understanding seemed to grow a lot, and they were accountable for their decisions. I would question everything. I wanted them learning, developing and understanding.

There are of course plenty of different types of questions to ask, as listed below:

Open	Closed
Leading	Probing
Combination	Challenging
Predictive	Summary

Whatever type of question you are using or looking to use, ask yourself the important questions first: What are players going to learn? How are they going to do it? Why do you need to know it?

6. Cues/Feedback

Along with questioning, the use of cues and feedback has become a popular method over the past few years. Allowing our players to play without interruption means that when breaks in play do occur (or you have to step in) coaches must get the feedback right. It is no longer a case of just telling players 'this is how it is'.

Advances in technology mean that players can watch video highlights of teams and individuals, and coaches often have apps they use with players during training and games. Whatever your preferred method of feedback - you must ensure your feedback is varied for different types of learning.

We often break our cues down into one of three areas: visual, auditory and kinaesthetic, the table below shows some ways in which feedback or cues within sessions can be put across:

Visual	Posters, pictures, whiteboards, videos, shape maps (formations), demonstrations.
Auditory	Group/paired/individual discussion, technical instruction.
Kinaesthetic	Demonstrations, freeze frames, half speed run through, waves, patterns of play rehearsal.

Although there are other forms of feedback, we tend to invest in the above three during our sessions because they are all closely linked to playing the game. Like questioning, it is less important that you know feedback is required; it is more important as to *why* you are selecting a specific form of feedback in the first place. In order to give feedback to players successfully you must understand how the person learns, you must understand what they respond to. This dictates not only the type but the timing of feedback and how often you give it.

Feedback will ultimately affect a player, whether it is positive or negative, and again it is down to the coaches to understand who can take what. Although positive feedback has a far greater positive effect on players' confidence and motivation levels, some players do, in fact, respond well to negative feedback; they see the feedback as 'learning' and as long as it is put across in a constructive manner, players will feed off of negative feedback too.

How are we challenging the person?

There is no doubt that we, as coaches, give our players advice, game-to-game and session-to-session, but we must go back to our planning stage to create sessions where advice and support are seen to provide a backbone, and players are given the freedom to express themselves in the time allocated to them.

When we create our sessions, they should be about challenging the intellectual understanding of the person during training - how can we get them to think about the game they play in a way that will aid development? Putting together the right type of session with a variety of methods to promote self-teaching is something we all need to focus on.

There are always going to be times when coaches have to take centre stage and show and tell players what they want. However, we must create sessions that ultimately allow players to learn for themselves. We are asking our players to adopt a 'style' that impacts positively on their lives; we are asking them to lead the 'type' of life that will allow them to have the best chance of being successful in football.

To challenge each player you must know them well enough to be able to take them out of their comfort zone but not so far as to put them off. It is a fine line to tread; one step too far and players will shut down, not enough and development is not going to occur.

As well as the different types of practices and methods, coaches must promote the fact that failure is a part of learning, in life not just in football. We must instil in our players the courage to go and fail in order to try new things that will ultimately help them develop. Sir Alex Ferguson stated that, "Failure isn't a problem, how you deal with it is the problem." Our players are looking at us to react when failure occurs, not as a footballer but as a person, and coaches, therefore, must (and I cannot stress this enough) react positively in the face of failure. If we are creating sessions that challenge individuals then *prepare for failure*. A lot of failure! Failure is okay.

Summary

There is a huge range of practices and methods that coaches can utilise to help players develop. Before deciding on particular approaches, though, it is important to understand your players and know what it is you are coaching (and why you are coaching).

All of us have different reasons for coaching, which will ultimately affect what and how we coach. What is important is that we are challenging our youth players in a range of different ways and that no matter how much failure occurs we embrace it and use it as positive reinforcement whenever possible. What players see from their coach has a huge bearing on whether they choose to try new things or not!

6. Things to think about

No matter how great the talent or efforts, some things just take time. You can't produce a baby in one month by making nine women pregnant. Warren Buffett

The final part of section one is dedicated to highlighting a range of things that coaches can think about when looking to move forward and develop young people and players. Like everything else in this world, we will not agree on everything and I simply offer the following as food for thought.

Suggestion 1 - Make football a lifestyle not a job

Football, as you know, is everywhere. From television to the web, we are inundated with resources - many of which other coaches have kindly taken the time to design and make available for us to use. With all this access to materials, game highlights, and opinions, we need to make our coaching a lifestyle activity and not simply a job. For many, you will know what I mean when I say - if you want to be successful, you must go above and beyond what others are currently doing.

If it means attending a local game to make new contacts then it is something that has to be done. If it means doing double the number of continued professional development (CPD) hours required for fully understanding a topic then that too is something that has to be done. You must eat, breathe, and live football. For some coaches, however, this is particularly difficult, especially if you have a full time job outside of football, as well as a family that you have to look after. However, part of development as a person is to do what you love and sacrifices sometimes have to be made. What I am really saying is, get rid of your family and friends and lose that job you hate, all for coaching football… I'm kidding! In fact, what I am really saying is if you want to coach, and if you want to be successful, you must *want* to develop yourself, which sometimes means you have to attend courses and seminars after normal working hours, trek around the country, make and take phone calls on Sunday evenings, and more!

Suggestion 2 - Be you! If you are not you, then who are you?

Above, it was highlighted how the vast number of resources available gives us variety and different options for coaching session plans on pretty much any topic we want. With this comes some great potential alternatives in your sessions and a chance to try a number of different approaches. There are now so many resources out there that we could just take someone else's ideas and apply them straightaway. In doing that, however, we may fail to recognise the subtle changes and differences that are needed for a particular group of players. A copy and paste approach makes us lazy coaches.

If you are looking to create your own coaching philosophy and have a good idea of how you want your teams to play and how best to develop the next generation of footballers, then it is important you only create what you want to see your teams doing. I have seen so many coaches who have virtually unlimited resources but absolutely no idea how they want their own teams playing and the team therefore lacks any kind of identity. If you want to develop your players, you must first decide on what journey you want to take them on. If you know your route then you can guide them effectively.

Suggestion 3 - A.P.P.L.Y

During my time coaching in Sydney, I was blessed to be given a fantastic opportunity to coach at Sydney University and had the chance to coach the Premier League's women's reserve team. It was the first real opportunity I was given to manage my own team properly and it was one I was determined to succeed at. I decided that I needed to create my own philosophy and base it on actions that I had to demonstrate, as well as my players. So I decided to settle on five key principles that I put into an acronym, that acronym was A.P.P.L.Y.

A = Attitude

The first aspect was 'attitude'. Attitude, for me, is something that can either make or break a person. Forgetting the football side, if you as a person do not have the right attitude then you will never develop.

Looking at how I wanted attitude to be demonstrated was simple. I wanted my team to demonstrate the kind of attitude that they would be proud of. Like my teaching, I judged the attitude of both my students and players alike on three key aspects:

1. Discipline – incorporating self-discipline on and off the training field and playing pitch. It is very important to instil discipline into anything you do and I wanted the players to recognise the need and importance of this. The act of 'being disciplined' can benefit so many other parts to one's life, such as time management, organisation, motivation, and concentration - so it was important for me to drive this forward at the earliest opportunity.

2. Respect – I wanted to see this demonstrated in the form of self-respect. Self-respect, though, is very difficult to actually teach a person, as you want the person to value their own existence, and have their own values and boundaries that they will not go below. In Sydney, this was (fortunately) easy due to the nature of the group and the age of my players but I feel it is important to recognise and have young players/people learning about, and understanding, self-respect at the earliest possible stage.

Too many people feel that respect is simply doing what you are told, being polite and not misbehaving, when in reality it is so much more. You must look to ask your players what they think it is, how it can be demonstrated, what it means to them in their homes (and their school), and how they can apply respect throughout their lives. Only when an individual understands how to respect themselves can they really begin to respect others.

3. Reliability – the final aspect that I included was reliability. Once I had instilled the two principles, above, it was simply about creating an environment where players recognised that they had to be reliant on themselves (and also on one another) in order to maximise their own development. I simply asked for the basics, to be able to turn up to training on time or early, give me their attention and effort in training and games, and look after one another throughout the season.

Although some would see these aspects as 'old school' – they are needed to succeed in anything that you do. I support many aspects of old school teaching, coaching, and learning - because they have been tried and tested. That is not to say that there aren't new methods that we should be doing; however, each of the three aspects complement one another. They come together to help create a person who is well on their way to developing themselves in any aspect of life. The right attitude is not a foolproof plan for success but without the right attitude, you are going to find it very difficult to succeed in anything. Coaches should have players discuss what attitude means to them and what behaviours they feel they should be demonstrating. Give players ownership and see what they can create for their own attitudes.

P = Posture

I wanted something to accompany attitude and that's where I brought in the concept of Posture. Although it is just one word, it incorporates many other aspects of what I want a team to demonstrate.

First and foremost, I wanted my players to look like football players: the way they stood, the way they moved and the way they conducted themselves. During training, I wanted my players in full training kit. During training I wanted my players stood up straight, I never wanted to see them slouching. I always explained that we would train the way we play and play the way we train, and if you trained like a slouch then you would effectively play like a slouch.

I wanted my players focused on what was happening, whether it was me giving instructions, a unit discussing a part of training, or just a general chitchat with teammates. All of this needed to stem from how they looked. I feel that it is key to look the part in order to play the part. Posture helps bring about professionalism and it was very important that players matched their attitude with how they carried themselves in order to play the part of a football player.

P = Possession

This aspect was the only 'footballing' principle I wanted to include in the fundamentals. I have felt extremely strongly about it ever since I started coaching. It was only really after watching my new team train 3-4 times that I immediately decided that the underlying goal of what I wanted to achieve during my time there was for the team to keep the ball better.

I would suggest, to any coach in the country, that the skill of maintaining possession in any area of the pitch should be fundamental to any team. It involves all of the basic fundamentals of individual technical skill and intelligence and impacts upon the structure and balance of a team.

L = Love

Another important factor that I wanted to put into my team was this aspect of Love. I wanted my players to love what they were doing and love the concept of getting together as a team to train and play. I wanted to create an environment that despite being autocratic (me being in charge), was one where they understood that 'no matter what' I would look after them whenever they were with me. Although old enough to take care of themselves, I wanted my players to feel that everything I did was for them and all I wanted them to do was develop as people and as players. How the love and togetherness developed across the team, over the entire season, was phenomenal to be a part of.

I would stress that no matter what level you coach at, you must create love around the team. Although this can sometimes be hard to do due to factors such as where players go to school (i.e. they may be rivals at school level) or different backgrounds (upper class vs. working class), we as coaches have a responsibility to educate these players to be part of something that brings people from different backgrounds and environments together. I believe this is a part of the game that, in recent times, has been forgotten.

Y = You

The final principle I included was 'You'; I wanted my players to understand that it was all about them. They were responsible for the way they trained and played, it was their effort, determination and will that was going to determine whether they would have a successful season or not. I wanted the players to know that if they applied themselves in the right way… they could achieve; I wanted that to come from them, not me.

As I told the players at the very last team talk I gave, at the end of a very successful season, they were the reason for their success. Although I had come in and instilled the philosophy, it was the players who decided to accept it and take on-board what I was asking them to do. I feel it is very important that giving credit is one of the best things you can do for a player but they must understand *why* they have been successful in *what* they have been doing.

I told my players, before I left, that I was the least important factor in the success of their season. I did so because I knew I would not be there next season and I did not want the success of the team to be attributed to something, or someone, that was no longer going to be present. For me, if you want to coach and be successful in what you do, you must convince the players that their development is in their own hands and you are there to guide and facilitate their development.

Although the application of A.P.P.L.Y. was a success for me, there is no guarantee it could work elsewhere or with another group of players. The obvious reasons for this are that the principles were applied to the set of players I had at the time. What I would encourage any coach to do, however, is create fundamental principles that you want to base your coaching around. Create the right type of environment that allows for development to take place. Then make your players (and any other staff) aware of this.

With A.P.P.L.Y. and my time in Sydney, not all players liked me. I am sure that many coaches reading this have come across players they just do not get on with (or whom they struggle with). Whether it is a clash of personalities, or you do not share the same outlook, you must create something that is first and foremost yours and something that you feel is going to develop players to the best of your (and their) abilities in order to move forward. Be okay with being different and unique as a coach.

Suggestion 4 - Plan, Prepare, and Prepare again

As stated, there is a lot of existing material out there that makes coaching a whole lot easier when planning sessions. Although we must use caution in how much we use, as we always want our sessions to be our own products, I would recommend that any coach builds up an armoury of what is known as 'core coaching sessions'. One advantage of creating these core sessions is that they can be repeated anytime throughout the season and can give your team the particular identify that you want them to have. Whether it is developing a possession-based team or a deep-lying counter attacking team, you must have your philosophy embedded in a range of core sessions.

As well as having these 'core' coaching sessions, we must be aware of the need for variation and change. This is where I feel we, as coaches, must be better educated by our governing body and clubs on how to actually write up and produce session plans geared very specifically towards certain games or tournaments that can feed from our own philosophies. This ability to write up detailed session plans (whether for grassroots clubs or Cat 1 academy sessions) is a brilliant skill to learn and something that although potentially time consuming can have some really positive effects on development.

In order to be able to write up detailed session plans you must firstly know your players; you must also have a good idea of how your opponents are likely to play. This generally occurs a lot more frequently in academy setups where coaches have the facilities and time to go through club styles and player profiling but it is also something that can done at the grassroots level and geared towards local and regional tournaments and cup games. Having to write a session plan that focuses on a strategy to be used in a cup game is highly educational for you as a coach and for your players. Showing the players the difference between sessions geared towards a cup game vs. a league game can aid player understanding and development of how you want them to play and train, and providing them with reasons why there are differences. This, I think, is a major area of development that we are still not taking on-board across the country but is something that, potentially, can aid development tenfold.

I would encourage coaches to think of the different ranges of scenarios that can occur and base training sessions on them. Below I have included a few scenarios, but *you* know your team, your players and your leagues; what scenarios often occur in league games, cup games and tournaments? How can you design a training session built for these?

Scenario one:

You have been drawn against a team in the third round of the regional cup (the game must be won on the day, goes to extra time and penalties) that you know very well. They have won the competition 3 out of the last 5 seasons in your age group and have always been a physically intimidating side. You have yet to play them in the league this season so it would be your first meeting. Understanding your players, how would you set the team up to play?

Scenario two:

You are in the final group game of your summer 7-a-side tournament. You have already qualified for the knockout stages of the tournament but the team you are facing need a win to ensure they go through with you. Understanding that the opposition is going to attack how could you ask your team to play? How could you have prepared them for this kind of scenario in the week prior to the tournament?

Suggestion 5 - Smile, it's only football ;)

Now do not take suggestion 5's title as suggesting that football isn't important; football is everything! Well to me it is anyway. What I mean by this is that no matter how important football is to you, your players, and those around you, you must always have some perspective on what you are trying to achieve.

A big mistake that a lot of coaches make, certainly at the grassroots level, is placing too great an emphasis on winning and forgetting what they are there to try and do - which is actually develop the player. It must be stressed, and I honestly cannot stress it enough, that winning means absolutely nothing in the younger age groups in football. I have coached kids and teams that have been beaten 15-0 and the players have come off sad, yet after a very short team talk they go off chasing their friends and smiling again. Resilience to failure is something I really admire in children. It is something that should be encouraged.

Of course, I am not saying failure on the whole is fine but coaches *must* be okay with failure occurring, a lot! Which is why I say to smile. Coaches must look to give children visual cues when trying and failing because without failure, learning cannot occur. We have all had the experience of a child turning around to either face the coach or parent when a mistake has been made and, more often than not, ended up with a disappointing look or negative communication from the coach or parent. We must put our own emotions to the side and encourage the types of emotions we want to see.

Suggestion 6 - If you want better technical players, give them a ball and teach them the basics

Being blunt, the English game has fallen short on producing top technical players for a few very simple and easily fixable reasons.

The first of which is the concept of 'size'. The size of a player is still a major factor when clubs decide whether to take on a player or keep a player. I have been involved in conversations with coaches at the elite level where they still point to the size of a player's parents, or the size of their feet. For what reason? It frustrates me to see players being overlooked because of their size or being put into a position that is dominated by 'bigger players'. Stop doing it! A person's size has no correlation to their ability levels and I can promise you it never will.

Is size advantageous? At times, maybe, but if you are actually basing the development of a football player on his or her physical attribute, which is something you have no control over, you may find that this does not lead to much success.

The second concept is 'athleticism'. Often linked to the size of a potential player, athleticism is seen as a fundamental part of being a successful footballer. But why? I am not saying for a second that football players do not need to be fit but I do question the ability of athletes to become footballers. Often individuals are brought into a team (grassroots or academy) who are physically developed and are played in mainly one of two positions, defender or striker. Why is this the case? Well often they are seen as either quick enough to catch a player who is through on goal, or, they are quick and strong enough to run through half a team with their pace and score. We often neglect most of the technical inadequacies of that type of player because of the physical attributes they have. This is not to say that it was the player's fault that the player got selected, and it is not to say the player wasn't / isn't / couldn't be a good player. But would nations such as Holland, Brazil, Germany or Spain select their players on a similar basis?

So what should we, as coaches, be selecting and developing? Well, not to sound patronising, but in order to play the game you need a ball. So how about we give players a ball and start from there? The F.A. has commented, through the EPPP, of the need to get players in the younger age groups working on technical aspects with a ball. So stop getting your teams to warm themselves up by going for a jog around the pitch. Look to create fun, technically-orientated warm ups that will ultimately get them physically warm anyway! Remember, if a player is not working with a ball then they are effectively becoming better cross-country runners.

Suggestion 7 - If you want to develop their understanding of the game, don't pigeon hole a player; let them find their position

Another key area where I feel a lot of coaches have failed the development of players, especially English players, is by not understanding the game of football. It often baffles me when I am told that players cannot play in a number of positions and players get pigeon-holed at 9 or 10 years old into a certain position. This unfortunately happens in the academy system as much as grassroots football - which is both surprising and worrying. I continuously demonstrate my frustration at this type of development and have often had many an argument on the matter. The way I explain it to players and coaching staff alike is like this:

'If you want to be a well developed person, be able to speak fluent English, read, write, learn how to speak another language such as French, be able to work out sums, or know the capital of Nepal - you don't simply go to English class and expect to understand everything else. You have to go to English, turn up to Maths, and sit and listen in Geography as well as French class. So if you want to understand the game of football, you must play in a number of positions... as varied as possible. And like developing as a person, you begin to learn what you are good at gradually over time, just like how you know what you are good at in school. Don't have a favourite subject in school, have 3 or 4, just like in football, love to play the game in a number of different positions'.

Although not the most scientific of explanations, I believe it gives the players and coaching staff an understanding of the importance of variety and adaptability. You only have to look at the Spanish national side over the past decade to see that any one of the front 5-6 players can effectively play in any position within the team, and play it well. It would be ludicrous to suggest that a player will be developed to the best of their ability if they have only ever played one or two positions. You only have to look at Gareth Bale now to see what a versatile player he is. It is no surprise to see that during his rise to fame (amongst other factors) he has effectively played in 4-5 positions on the pitch in both the Premier League and La Liga. He is getting first-hand experience, and learning and gaining a greater understanding of the game, through different positions and outlooks on the pitch.

Suggestion 8 - Scientific research is wonderful, but don't get bogged down by it

My final suggestion is to do with research and books. Aside from the obvious contradiction of reading this book, it is important not to get bogged down by all the science and mass of literature that is available to us. Initially, I was a huge fan of the academic side of sport and always felt that research was the key to unlocking the door to potential.

However, through my studies and I am sure like many of yours, you begin to recognise that, although research can be a fantastic thing, much of it cannot be applied. So take what research is out there and read it, think about it, and apply it as appropriate - but remember, research doesn't create players, you do.

7. Developing the person – Why is this just as important?

Nothing will work unless you do. John Wooden

This next section looks at a different perspective of youth development, a perspective that so many coaches, clubs, and governing bodies forget about. In reality, it is just as, if not more, important as the football side of development. It is *developing the person*.

In this part to the book, we will look at the issues and potential solutions that can be used to further aid our development of youth players. For too long, football in this country has been a decade behind in its development process compared to that of other top nations within the game. It has even got to the stage where football isn't our most developed sport. Other sports have taken onboard new methods of training, new technologies, and most notably, a new culture and approach to youth development.

What's been the problem?

Times have changed and are continuing to change. Society is very different to what it was only ten years ago, and children are being brought up under today's norms. So what's the problem? I mean we have more qualified coaches than ever before, we have more facilities than were available in the past (although many of us can't use them), and there is more coverage of football on television and the internet than ever before. Exposure to football alone should work, shouldn't it?

Unfortunately, exposure to more football just isn't the answer. Having our EPPP auditors tell us that an U14's age group at academy level should be completing at least five hours of football a week just isn't the cultural development we need in this country. Our development needs to be looked at from a personal, deeper perspective.

I am a true believer (maybe one of few) in the simple fact that England cannot take something another nation such as Spain, Holland, or Germany has done and replicate it. To me it just doesn't make sense. For all the tiki taka, expansive high line pressing, and counter-attacking-at-pace football we have seen from these nations, it is not so simple that we can see it, replicate it, and fit it into our football. Factors outside football just do not permit it. England may be going some way towards trying to change this with the creation of the new English DNA (that outlines how English players should play) and it would be wrong to say that we cannot learn from other successful nations - but it is essential that we make something of our own.

Too many factors within our society - including the way we are brought up, the culture, the education system, and the general way we live, do not allow us to bring something from somewhere else and make it work. Well, not on the scale we want it to work anyway. Take obesity levels as an example. Public Health England reported that almost a third of 10-11 year olds and over a fifth of 4-5 year olds are overweight or obese. This has been attributed to factors such as the school food children eat (Jamie Oliver's school food campaign noted), as well as access to facilities. Sky Sports reported through their 'grassroots survey' that 84% of the footballing community felt that facilities were still an issue and that lack of investment underpinned this. With the recent financial downturn and belt-tightening - some families have struggled to pay for grassroots coaching which affects the development or at least opportunity for young players to play.

Who are the youth of today?

The youth of today are very different from generations of old; they are a new breed, no better, no worse, just different. They have been born into a time when technology is the norm, where answers to questions and problems can be solved with a click of a few buttons and where social interaction and acceptance can be gained without a word being spoken. It makes the development of our footballing youngsters a much tougher job for coaches and clubs because we are dealing with a generation that really has not been seen before.

When I look at the youth as a whole, I see a mixture of personalities; these drive a number of the behaviours listed below:

- Curious
- Inquisitive
- Closed off
- Shy
- Anxious
- Reluctant
- Creative
- Misguided
- Technologically Sound

Some of these traits can make coaching a challenging time for any person. If we are unable to relate to, and get to know, the players as people then we have very little chance of developing them.

A lot of what might be construed as 'negative' traits occur because we have a culture that is frightened to fail. This is demonstrated in our education system as well as our football and it can often cause our youths to shut down and refuse to even try. This then requires time, patience and the understanding of teachers, coaches, parents and friends to draw the young person out. Not all influential people are positive in a young person's life.

The above is, of course, not true of all young people. However, I ask myself how many potential players and good people are we missing out on because we do not take the time to get to know the person behind who we are coaching.

What are we missing?

I always seem to have a conversation, at some point, with other coaches (especially at the grassroots) that leads to the statement of, *'We only have an hour to work with our players, so there is only so much we can do to help improve them as players'*. Although time is a limiting factor in many ways, you can still get to know your players. Whether a player is five years old and telling you about how much they love sliding in the mud (with every second word being an 'erm'), or it's a 16 year old academy player who is likely to get a two year scholarship at a Championship club, you must effectively treat them with the same amount of attention, respect and interest as each other or anyone else.

It is here that I feel our major failings occur as coaches, and we are probably one of the most influential set of people that any young person is likely to come into contact with. It is of the utmost importance, therefore, that you aim to take an interest in every player that you come across; find out their likes, dislikes, strengths and weaknesses, as a person not as a player. Some of us may do this with questionnaires at the start of the season, but more often than not, we do this for training purposes, not simply because we want to know and want to build a rapport with them.

We are essentially missing the nurturing and mentoring side to the coaching process (which will be discussed later in the book), which is just as important as the coaching of techniques and skills. Although we are employed to create better players, coaches, like teachers and many other professionals, have a higher moral duty of care for each individual and I believe this higher duty of care should not come as an obligatory part of your job role, but instead it should be part of who you are.

I have seen, far too many times unfortunately, coaches (within grassroots and academies) who simply do not enjoy getting to know their players. Yet because they have a range of qualifications related to football, they are put in charge of a group that often they do not want. This creates a huge problem in the sense that coaches will never look to go 'above and beyond' for their players and players inadvertently will then demonstrate the same behaviour. The basic care, love and respect for the person doesn't come out and our young players suffer because of it.

What have we been setting the person up for?

Essentially, what we, as coaches, are trying to do is prepare our youth for the world of potential professional football. However, we should not be naive to the fact that the number of players who actually make a full and long lasting career in football is very small indeed. Anderson and Miller (2011) highlighted this simple but brutal fact:

For many young players, their career as a top footballer is potentially over at 16 or 18... fewer than 10% of those who turn professional actually play more than 50 matches for their home team.

In this, we are talking about 16-18 year olds as youth, and by this age it is very difficult to adjust and develop a person to be able to deal with the failures they are likely to see while playing football and competing for contracts. The reason why it is often so difficult is because the upbringing has solely been based on the development of the player, they have often travelled through academies from a young age to be told they didn't make the final cut. Very little gets spoken about around other elements of their lives.

Within this, I feel that clubs as well as organisations such as the F.A., the Football League, the Premier League and the PFA need to recognise is that although football is the dream and drive for most young people, the need to recognise the importance of other areas like education, personal development through life skills (manners, discipline, respect, etc.) should be part of a frame that (at present) just isn't there. The PFA, for example, provides a service which is good to see. However, it is often geared towards careers within coaching in the game for players who may have been tossed out of football only months before.

Certain organisations within football behave reactively when it is often already too late (e.g., for when players fail to obtain a professional contract). More often than not, it is too late to be looking to instil new things into players who run the risk of being filled with disappointment, anger and frustration. Resilience and grit are not words that are often used around the youth of today; their upbringing is vastly different and at times can appear far more comfortable than previous generations. However, it is these kinds of mindsets that need to be instilled at a very young age in order to develop a person to deal with the demands that football places on players and people.

It is clear, at present, that the upbringing of our youth as people do not give them the best chances to succeed. Anderson and Miller added that even the football environment within this country struggle to cope with the change in demands of our young players. It is commented how many of the players that make it into the reserve game, will (still) struggle to adapt and progress to meet the demands of the first team. Many will drop off at this point. Many, of course, will say that the attitude was spot on and commitment couldn't be questioned but they just couldn't meet the standard. That standard is often linked to the person's ability to adapt, understand (through game understanding and intelligence), and deliver what is required. These attributes can of course be taught and developed but they need to be done with the person from a young age.

It is here that really we as a nation, clubs, and coaches should be asking: what are we trying to create and what are we setting our players up for? It should not be difficult to understand that good habits, morals, values should be instilled as early as possible and many clubs and coaches do this really well. However, the values we bring to our clubs should be values that reflect what their parents are trying to instil (or should be instilling) and how schools operate because if people only have to demonstrate these values in one area of their lives then habits are not going to be formed.

What needs to change?

I believe that in order to successfully develop youth players we must look beyond football alone. Yes, of course, coaching skills, tactics, and game understanding are all essential to develop top players. However, in order to be a top professional there must be something more; the person must recognise the demands of the game from a 'whole' perspective and not just feel they need to meet the demands of football. This often comes down to what people (as players) are willing to do beyond the training pitch.

I feel that in order to develop good young hungry players you need to develop every part of the individual. This is not always down to the coaches but clubs and national organisations must look to include those around young players and make parents, family, friends, and schools aware of just how important their contributions are to the development of players in this country. People must understand the value of the *process* of development and not just gaze at the odd outcome or prove reactive to negative outcomes that are then very difficult to change.

Summary

Creating the right type of person to be successful in the game of football goes well beyond the training pitch. The need for coaches, parents, clubs and national organisations to pay far more attention to the personal details of development is essential if we are going to improve the number of top quality young players we produce.

This goes as far down as the need to teach and instruct appropriate appearance, values, and education – all with the goal in mind that whatever the outcome of a young player's career (either a long lasting career or one that ends at 18) we should be confident in knowing that the person will not only be able to deal with footballing demands but can be prepared to excel in other important areas of life.

The following chapters of this book look at a range of topics that can have a huge impact on the development of the person (education, life skills, influences of others). We must begin to recognise the needs and importance of personal development in all areas of life that can look to benefit footballing performance to give our young players the best chance of making the career they want.

8. Does talent exist? Are we pigeon-holing people?

Hard work beats talent when talent fails to work hard. Tim Notke

The above quote is one that so many coaches (including myself in the past) have used when trying to instil improvements in a player's work ethic, motivation, and even inspiration. We want our players to work hard, but doesn't that mean we are telling them that they are not 'talented'? Or are we saying that all of our players are 'talented', but still have to work hard? It's a strange saying, when I look back on it now. In fact, nowadays I consciously steer away from any talk where the word 'talent' is involved.

Talent and its issues

For me the word talent defines 'someone who consistently demonstrates a high level of skill in a particular field, whether it is football, mathematics or dance'. I could go on for an entire book about talent and whether it exists or not but there are fantastic books such as *Bounce* and *The Talent Code,* amongst others, that go into far greater depth than I ever could. All I will say is that I am not a believer that 'talent' exists and it's not as simple as some people having it and others not having it.

I have in the past asked the following questions when talent has cropped up in discussions, particularly with regard to genetics: How many major tournaments did Tiger Woods' father win? How many Champions League medals does Lionel Messi's father have? How many teams did Jose Mourinho's father win domestic leagues with?

Do we pigeonhole People?

For a long time, football discussions have centred around players having 'talent'. It was something that we couldn't explain and we marvelled at how certain individuals could seemingly do things that others couldn't. However, more recently, people have come to the general consensus that top players are not created due to inherent talent, but how they work and how they train. Sport science developments have had a huge impact over the last decade in helping to create world-class players.

There remains, however, pigeonholing in football. Is a player good enough? Either he has it or he doesn't. This can be seen when organisations, clubs and coaches call 'talent identification' meetings to discuss what they are looking for. The concept humours me because, effectively, young players who have an acceptable level of skill are being judged and yet coaches, scouts, and managers often have no idea what the young player has done to get to that level.

Top clubs are now recruiting 5-6 year olds, and claiming to have some of the most talented youngsters in the country. The word talented or gifted seems to have become part of our subconscious football language and often appears in national organisations, manuals, and seminars!

Where I feel talent actually comes from

Malcolm Gladwell wrote a fantastic book called *Outliers* in which he presented the '10,000 hours of practice' concept. In turn, many of us have read it and probably delved deeper into the work of Anders Ericsson who first developed the notion of how 10,000 hours of purposeful practice equates (on average) to expert level performances. Our youth modules have taught us the importance of allowing as much playing time as possible to enable players to progress and develop.

Despite the value of 10,000 hours, Gladwell still believed that talent was a naturally occurring thing, and Ericsson, like myself, disagrees with this. The reason behind such disagreement is that although he acknowledges the concept of purposeful practice Gladwell has expressed the 'old school vision' of talent existing when no research has claimed to find what talent actually is in individuals. There is no set formula for footballers who are talented vs. those who are apparently not.

This is not to say that once ten thousand hours of practice has been achieved that you *automatically* become an expert in your field, far from it. Although the need for purposeful practice is essential in the development of a young footballer's career, there are several other important factors that must be dealt with in order to reach a consistent higher level of performance. Environment, coaches, personal attitude and mentality all have an important role to play.

Take the New Zealand rugby team; the most successful national side in the world underwent a distinct change and adaptation to their culture. In his book *Legacy*, the author, James Kerr, described how factors such as coaches' behaviour, personal attitude and development created a new mentality to develop not only great players but also great people. The 15 key lessons discussed in the book were shaped around the notion of developing environments and cultures to create leaders. Here, all of this doesn't just come to be; I do not believe it is simply made from nothing. Instead, the above areas all have contributing factors that lead to players with higher abilities on and off the pitch.

British cycling went through a similar phase, employing a whole new team to revolutionise the GB setup, adapting environments and methods of training, employing a mindset that focused on individuals (delivered by Dr Steve Peters, writer of *The Chimp Paradox*) and being the best they could be. There was no acceptance that talent would pull these teams through; instead, hard work, cultural changes and expert input were key to success.

In football, take the example of Frank Lampard, signed for a large sum of money (well, £11million was at the time) by Chelsea. Lampard came into a squad with many questioning whether he deserved to be there and what he could offer. There was no doubt he had potential, he came from a West Ham youth system that had produced the likes of Joe Cole and Jermaine Defoe around the same period and which was regarded as one of the best youth academies in the country. However, was he a player that would seemingly walk into the Chelsea team? Was he already a star player? Most certainly not.

What changed was the fact that Frank Lampard had come into a whole new environment. With all due respect to West Ham, Chelsea, who were taken over by the Russian Billionaire Roman Abramovich had higher expectations within the Premier League and in Europe than West Ham. With the revised mentality at the club, Lampard's own mentality changed. He was put into an environment that allowed him (amongst others) to grow and develop into the player we now rate as one of the best midfielders the Premier League has ever seen. This environment was built on the expectations and standards set out by the club and by Lampard's coaches. Both Claudio Ranieri and Jose Mourinho had a huge influence on how he trained; his training regime changed as well as his positioning around the pitch, his environment was one filled with new learning and development opportunities, which built his game understanding.

Sir Chris Hoy hosted a 2014 programme on the BBC called *How to win Gold* and offered an informative and insightful look into what it takes to be successful in sport. Using his own experience, Sir Chris took us through how he came to be the most successful British Olympian of all time, and what he made very clear from the outset is that it had nothing to do with talent.

Instead, he attributed his success to 'opportunity' (facilities to practice and train), and the support of his parents who used to drive him to competitions when he was young (which allowed him the sufficient time to practice). He commented on the positive influence of certain teachers in his school and how he was given time to practice and train. He then discussed how the team he had around him (throughout the competitions he raced in) were an essential part to his success. He also gave great credit to Dr Steve Peters, in changing his psychological outlook on competition, and also highlighted the importance of technological advances in sport science, nutrition and lifestyle.

Ultimately, what you gain from Sir Chris's story is that it is a collection of key areas that must all work, in sync, in order for development to take place. Even down to the smallest details. Shane Sutton, who was one of the cycling coaches Hoy worked with commented that each cyclist would have their own mattress made for them so that they would feel like they were sleeping in their own beds to aid recovery and allow cyclists to get a better sleep. This was done when they were on the road, during competitions; Sir Bradley Wiggins had his bed follow him through the stages of the Tour de France. When it got broken down throughout the hour-long programme, you could see that talent was the last thing anyone attributed to the success of Sir Chris Hoy.

This was not to say that Hoy did not have skill. He demonstrated his ability in training, in the sport science labs, and during competition. He showed he had what it took to be a champion. His desire and motivation were second to none but it required all of the above to work together in order for him to be successful within his sport.

What is so important in developing the person is that we work together (as coaches, parents, and teachers) to provide the right opportunities, facilities, training, and mindset needed to be successful.

Some coaches may say: well that player just doesn't get it; he/she hasn't got the talent for it. Here are some questions I would fire back:

1. Did you try coaching that player in a different way (visual, auditory, kinaesthetic)?
2. How much ownership did the player(s) have over what they were doing?
3. Did you coach the player or the person?
4. What is the actual issue? Is it technical, tactical, social, psychological, physical? (Many coaches often cannot see what the underlying problem is).
5. How long has the issue persisted for? (sometimes time is all a person needs)

The major point that I feel coaches need to get past, with regards to talent (and whether you believe in the concept of it or not), is that you do not use it as an excuse for a player not making it as a professional in football or any other profession. By using the phrase 'he/she wasn't talented enough' we are almost giving ourselves an excuse, when realistically there are a hundred different reasons as to why someone may not have made it.

How does the concept of talent affect the development process of young people?

I watched a television programme recently on Channel 4 called *Child Genius*. Twenty young prodigies were tasked with a number of mental, memory, and academic challenges to determine who the smartest child in Britain was. I watched in amazement at the lengths some parents would go to in order to see their child succeed. For example, some would provide them with 'brain food' prior to tests, make them study extensively after school (at such a young age), create an after school extracurricular schedule, and dominate the decision-making. It was all a bit over the top to be honest.

Amongst all the great child minds (and their parents... who were more worried about winning than the child most of the time), there was one individual that really stood out, one little girl called Jocelyn. Only 8 years old, and someone who had never gone to school, she showed remarkable development for someone so young. Her parents explained that she didn't go to school because she simply didn't want to, and that the environment, which was based around curriculums and tests, was not somewhere she wanted to be. Instead, she was home schooled and she learnt about the things she wanted to learn about. Her mother gave one example of how they spent four hours on a trampoline, learning about sharks.

The most remarkable thing about this young girl was not her super 'intelligence', she actually went out in the first round after struggling in the mathematics and memory tasks of the competition. What was inspiring and amazing was to see just how happy this little girl was.

For a child who had never been in a competitive environment and who had never been tested on her intelligence before, I felt she did remarkably well. What was even more delightful was to see how she reacted to failure. After the first round of the competition (maths), she laid crying in her mother's arms, obviously disappointed in her performance, yet in the second round she actively went skipping out of the testing hall. That was down to the feedback and nurturing of her parents. Upon returning from the competition, she took it upon herself to write a poem about the competition. No one forced her, there was no scheduling of task and teaching time, she chose to do it all by herself.

This is not to say that all children should be home schooled, it takes a great amount of time, patience and academic and life knowledge (and experience) from parents to be able to teach their child. However, Jocelyn seemed the happiest and brightest young child I had ever seen.

The *Child Genius* programme links into the development of our young players and young people. Coaches should look to ask their players one question: what would they like to learn in today's session? It's a scary concept because it goes against all that we have learned and prepared for as coaches. I mean failure to prepare is preparing to fail, right? We have spent hours putting together sessions to aid the development of our players; we are coaching things and teaching our players what they need to know, right?

Well how about you ask a player what they want to know, ask a team where they feel they are going wrong on the pitch, ask a captain how they feel about leading a session. These things help development because you are providing ownership. I watched this programme with little Jocelyn sitting in a room full of books just reading, no mother and father bearing down; she was just reading because she wanted to. Would her knowledge of words, storytelling, and imagination improve from this? Of course it would. And who was telling her to do it? No one. She was in charge of her learning and she decided what she wanted to learn.

Coaches must be brave when developing players. Sometimes stepping away from the standardised method of coaching and learning is frightening, I know, but what can be created in the long run could be wonderful. Not only are you likely to see development but you will see a desire from players to learn more, to want to be pushed more, and *that* is where we can then step in and help. It's certainly not about putting on fancy sessions with progressions and challenges and cones and flat discs when players have no input and therefore no real reason to learn. There will certainly be times when children will need order, discipline and structure; however, they will also need chaos, freedom and fun to balance it all out.

What I learned from that programme, and how I saw development, was not about seeing and watching naturally talented children; instead I looked at Jocelyn and witnessed a young girl spending hours of purposeful practice and learning about things she enjoyed. Her ability to retain information, I feel, was not down to being talented but because she took an active interest in what she was doing. It was fun and she wanted to do it. We as coaches must be looking to engage our players far more to enable them to spend sufficient time carrying out purposeful practice with the goal of giving freedom, ownership, and choice into what they learn about football.

Summary

Whatever your view on talent is, be mindful of how you use its terminology. To state a player 'isn't talented enough' is something that needs to be lost. We are at a stage where we have the resources, facilities and understanding such that we can always have a positive impact on the development of a young player's future. There are very few excuses for us not being able to create a positive highly skilled player for the future game.

There may well be reasons behind players not making it into the professional game. The quicker we get away from using talent as an excuse the quicker we can concentrate on identifying and rectifying issues that could affect the development of young players. And the quicker we are likely to see the creation of top young homegrown players in this country.

9. How mainstream education affects us developing the person

The best teachers are those who show you where to look, but don't tell you what to see.
Alexandra Trenfor

Many of us are fully aware of the shortcomings that affect the development of young homegrown players. However, the F.A. isn't the only large organisation that struggles to lay out a successful model for the production of top young players. The education system in this country has a huge influence on football both in and out of school, and contributes to continuing issues when developing young people.

We need to stop looking at the development of our young people being confined to the classroom and need our schools to educate our young people about things outside the classroom too. We live in a world that requires us to almost start again with young people, to re-educate life skills in them, to make them appreciate education in order to live a better life regardless of what they do with it. Only when the cohesion between football and education is tightly knit can you begin to fully develop top young players and people.

Current state of affairs in education

The education system as a whole has developed into a very 'corporate' environment, especially at the higher end and has been gradually filtering its way down the system.

In primary schools, we see young children and young players learn through 'doing'; they are part of an environment that promotes expression and creativity. This is what we try to create within coaching sessions as well, therefore complementing a primary school programme of development.

High/Secondary schools, however, focus on targets, gearing pupils' learning and memorising for exams, taking away – at times – the means to express themselves, taking away time for trial and error and creativity. It has also led to more and more students (and therefore our young players) lacking certain key skills such as basic functional skills and personal skills including listening, communicating, presenting and leadership.

We now see large numbers of young people withdrawn from the 'experience' side of development, due to the advancement of technology and social media, alongside issues within general society (no ball games, lack of playing facilities, increase in crime rates, safeguarding, etc.).

How is education affecting the footballer?

When I look at the development of young people and young players I look at a number of key elements that I feel will help me learn about each person individually when I first meet them; they are as follows:

1. How they shake my hand
2. Do they look me in the eye when talking to me
3. How they interact with others during an ice-breaking session
4. Body language (open vs. closed posture)
5. How they deal with failure (created by myself)

All of the above elements have absolutely nothing to do with 'academic' education whatsoever, yet they can shape how I feel a person will learn and what I need to do in order to get them to succeed. For a footballer this is even more important, the basic elements of what I look for in those five areas are: respect, focus, communication, positivity and determination, all essential characteristics needed for footballing success. These are what we will often call developing life skills.

The education system has never traditionally looked to actively teach life skills in schools nor help instil the fundamentals mentioned above. How do you expect a young player to get up and hustle for a ball given away if failure links to disappointment and neglect in schools? How would you expect a player to focus and pay attention when they have been removed from a class for being disruptive and left to their own devices? How can you teach a player about discipline when they are allowed to participate in sports for their school even though their behaviour in a class has been poor or homework has not been completed?

The inconsistency of rules and regulations between football and school often means a young player can pretty much lead two separate lives as long as they are seen to have the necessary skills to play at a good level. There should be a clear linear relationship in rules, regulations and communication between player, parents/family, schools and football clubs.

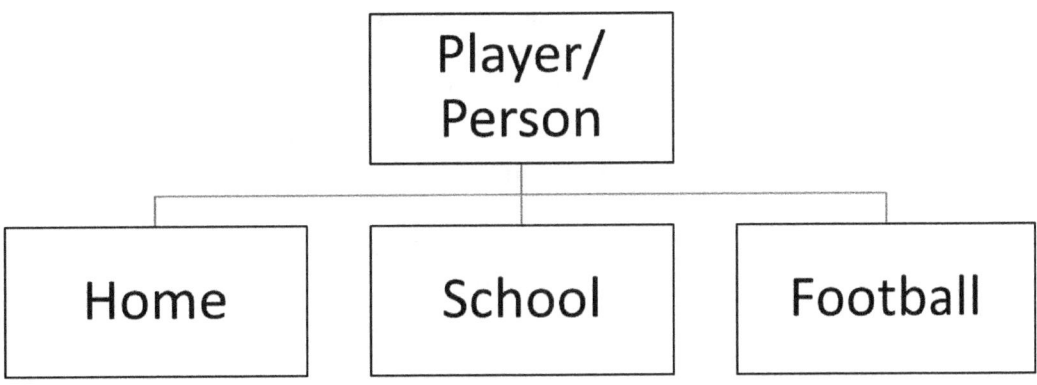

The unfortunate and sad truth is that, at present, there is little to no relationship between these three influential environments and this can have a huge impact on a player's development. I actually spoke to personnel within a football club in England who believed: *"If things happen in school then it's not our problem, let the school deal with it."* I was in shock, I could not understand how they failed to see the relationship between school and the club and the importance of everyone singing from the same hymn sheet.

This is not to say that such attitudes are reflected at every club. I recently spoke to the head coach of a development squad who stated the importance of education and how it relates to football performance, he said:

"If you can do something you feel you may hate, with the same enthusiasm, dedication and attention as something you love, then you will be successful."

This is something that needs to be instilled in young players. Parents, teachers and coaches should be highlighting the importance of each other's professions and relating everything a young player does back to all three areas (home, school, football).

What do players need from their schools?

Ultimately, what we are looking for in our schools is the ability to engage our young players as people. This means providing the understanding that being a top class football player requires more than technical ability. Below are a set of recommendations that can (and, in my opinion, should) be put in place by schools that can aid the development of not only the player but the young person as well.

Student-Athlete codes of conduct

Firstly, young players need to be given a clear set of rules and regulations to follow. Although schools will have their own student code of conduct, it is a good idea to develop a student-athlete code of conduct for all individuals that represent and play sport for their schools. Here you are acknowledging the fact that people may have high levels of skill in one or more sports, however what you are also making clear is how, with that skill, there comes an added responsibility to be a role model.

These young people represent their schools and as such should be deemed responsible enough to adequately and positively act for themselves and the school they are competing for. Here schools can get local grassroots or elite clubs involved in the process, asking for their rules/codes of conduct to create consistency with young players. Areas such as attendance and punctuality, dress code, behaviour, and homework completion, can all be targeted.

Key areas should be communicated in a way that echoes the need for individuals to excel and progress in academia in order to compete for their schools. Actual academic grading or marking should be discouraged from being in any code of conduct (for example, they must maintain C grades and above) because you are putting undue pressure on someone to maintain standards in something they may genuinely struggle with. If the central focus of the code of conduct is focused on being a positive role model (and this is echoed by parents, schools and clubs), you are then going some way towards helping a young player develop the necessary skills to achieve success.

Incorporate life skills development into a sporting curriculum

A huge ask but I am sure you would agree that incorporating life skills into schools should be fundamental if we are to engage and develop young people. A more formal approach to developing essential life skills in areas such as emotional intelligence, core beliefs and values, empathy, mindset, etc., should be delivered in all secondary schools around the country.

Some programmes (e.g. Skills for Life, Life Skills) have begun to make life skills more accessible but schools should take on the responsibility of developing them once young people begin secondary school. Once young people enter secondary school, they are exposed to teenagers (while becoming one themselves) and an environment that can be seen as a lot more demanding socially as well as academically. If schools are able to use football (as well as other sports) as a base to teach young people about personal development then they can aid in the development of the person as well as the player.

Incorporate football development days into a sporting curriculum

Here I feel the F.A., as well as local and elite clubs, should be given the opportunity to put on workshops for young people and have players talk to them about a range of topics that link to development. There are some fantastic coaches and coach educators in England who could have a great impact on young people when talking about things such as a club's culture, how players need to buy into it, and the need for those players to achieve in school, be respectful, etc. You only have to look at some of the materials created and distributed around Twitter to see just how much educational thinking goes into coaching these days and the depth of what we are asking of our young players.

It is also clear that coaches cannot achieve all of it during footballing contact time. As such, clubs as well as schools should take responsibility for educating young players as to the importance of their education in relation to football performance and progression. Allocating time slots to help impact positively on young players and their progression is key and can often reinforce what schools are telling their students.

What do players need from their coaches?

As well as schools needing to change and adapt to help promote the development of young players and students, individual coaches around the country have a key part to play in the overall development of a person. It is no longer enough to allow young players to lead separate lives (in school and in football) – there should be one mindset throughout. Clubs must recognise this, and the need to carry out education must filter down to all coaches (whether in elite or grassroots clubs).

Provide positive educational experiences

Coaches need to be a positive force in players' lives. One way this could be done is to relay positive educational experiences that you may have had in the past and explain why they have helped you. Whether it is in maths, geography, or anything else, providing players with positive versions of education can go some way towards getting them to understand education's value. As coaches, we cannot make our players love education (although a lot do and this should be celebrated) but you can provide and share consistent experiences.

An example might be achieving an award (head boy/girl, achieving a good test score, an attendance/punctuality award) in anything in school and commenting on why that is a positive aspect a player should be proud of. This can be communicated during a warm up or cool down when a group is together. Players will feed from coaches and if coaches are seen to be raving about education, it can only be a positive thing.

Ask basic questions

Another thing a coach can do is ask very basic questions about a school day to demonstrate a genuine interest in what players do (and all coaches should be genuinely interested!). Questions such as:

- How was school? – look for more than a one word answer; for example, if a player says 'fine', I normally ask, 'why was it fine? And why wasn't it great?'

- What lessons did you have today?

- Tell me three things you learned today while in school?

- What are your favourite subjects and why? – try not to focus too much on P.E., as being directed back to sport can often overshadow other important lessons.

At times, we may feel a bit uncomfortable asking questions about school because some of us may not have come from an academic background and questioning may feel a bit alien. However, like anything else it is about practice and trialling what questions bring out the right type of answers. The point of questioning in this instance is not always to get a particular answer but rather to get an insight into what your players may enjoy and why. You'll often find that you can use some things in a positive way during training and games from the answers you get.

Ask parents/guardians for reports and updates

Another avenue is to have the parents/guardians of players give you regular feedback about their school lives. This can often interlink well if a school has a strict code of conduct (or has managed to develop an individualised student-athlete code of conduct). All coaches should be looking to be aware of any issues a player is having at school in order to provide support for both the player and their parents/guardians. Coaches should strive to encourage a positive outlook on education by players *and parents* and should players find things difficult (or are in trouble) coaches should be reiterating what parents are telling their children.

Generate a traffic light system with behaviour

One way to promote positive behaviours in school is to incorporate a traffic light system where any form of misbehaviour or poor attitude will result in an equal punishment to what the school has provided. Each club and each coach can create their own unique versions but an example system may look like the following:

Green Light – this could be a minor incident such as receiving detention in school, which can result in parents notifying a coach who then speaks to the player (or club official such as lead phase coach) about the need to be positive in school.

Yellow Light – here a more serious form of discipline taken by the school (such as a prolonged detention over a number of weeks or a suspension from school) may mean that both coach and club discuss with parents possible footballing consequences such as: the player is not allowed to train, or can train but cannot play in games until punishments have been completed. Here coaches and clubs should support any parent's decision (such as not allowing their son/daughter to train). Having a number of options as a coach and club can help promote positive behaviour in schools.

Red Light – here a young person may have been excluded from school. As rare as this is, coaches and clubs should still have a process in place to follow. Again, liaising with the parent is essential but a coach may decide that the player doesn't train or play until he/she is back in a new school and demonstrates a positive approach. It may even mean removing the player from the club. Again, this is extremely rare but making all players aware of how seriously you, as a coach, take education will hopefully go some way to helping players understand the importance of school.

The key point behind this system is not to just punish a player, but instead help them realise that actions have consequences in all areas of life. Sometimes a player may just need a talking to in order to help them learn and understand the reasoning behind something. At other times though, there may need to be a serious consequence to make a player realise what they did/or are doing will not benefit any kind of positive future. Bring football and education together.

What responsibilities do we all have?

Education should be, in part, about teaching our youngsters about the bigger picture in life. There is no doubt that understanding won't be achieved by all people, however, a *consistent* effort to make people aware of what they can achieve should be at the forefront of discussions and debates in classes across the country. Again this is something that should be echoed in clubs and only through effective communication (that many of us teach – on the pitch – to our players) with schools can this be achieved.

This, you often find, will lead to schools and teachers giving students more responsibility and ownership over their own futures. Again, these are not academic skills but life skills and they cannot become good habits if not used, tweaked and enhanced on a regular basis in a range of different environments. This is why we must challenge coaches, teachers and parents to be consistent (not always easy I know) with what we do.

Finally, and probably most importantly, young players need to be seen to actively involve themselves in school. We want them to develop effective personal skills and become role models for good behaviour and attitudes as early as possible. By giving responsibility to young people, schools have a better chance of engaging with them and teaching them the skills that they can take forward into their training and games, and which will benefit them as players.

Summary

The education system has a lot to make up for when looking at the development of young people in this country. Change is unlikely to occur en masse at the top of the pyramid so it is important for individuals, departments, schools and clubs to see the value in educating our young people in the right way.

It must be seen that education doesn't always mean academic success for the sake of funding, but instead seeks to develop essential life skills. This is something that football clubs all over the country need to take far more of an interest and active role in - if they want to produce top homegrown players for the future game.

10. Academic Education vs. Life Education

Education is not preparation for life: Education is life itself. John Dewey

This chapter has been motivated by my experience of teaching and coaching young people (both in the classroom and on the training pitch) and my observations of the differences between generations.

Academic education is something I see young people rarely valuing and I wanted to reflect on what I felt was needed to succeed. I am a big believer in education, not necessarily the education that we are provided with by schools in the UK, but life education and how we need to take advantage of education every single day. I would hope that many of us recognise this type of education and encourage it.

Young players, like young people, need to understand that education is not confined to a classroom; it is not about achieving an A grade and it is not about passing exams. Education is the development of knowledge and application that will allow that person to live a better life. Something I fear we forget to instil in our young footballers.

Academia for a Player

During my studies, many years ago, I was asked to complete an assignment that reflected upon how 'we' (as teachers) felt students perceived education. It was a very interesting question and something I thought about for a long time. Finally, I wrote my assignment and began with this opening paragraph:

'I am mere mortal; expectation means nothing to me, for I am only human. I myself cannot change the world and therefore have no control. I do not choose my future, my path; it is already laid out before me, I cannot make positive changes because life does not allow me to do so, it pulls me down, so all I must do is survive, this is my life and who I must be, not what I want but who am I to say or do otherwise? There are great minds in the world, far greater than mine, yet the world is not a great and powerful place, and if they cannot create change in this world, who am I to suggest I can even make the slightest difference? Who am I to stand up and say I can change this world? Who am I?'

I know! Rather extravagant and over the top but I had my academic head on! What I went on to say was that students within academic education often find themselves lost (not all of course... some know what they want and some know they are going to university or straight into work). For the majority, though, education and academic qualifications are now a thing that everyone seems to have, a degree means very little, a Masters only a little bit more. Ultimately, employers want experience but only with a qualification if you want to survive in the working world.

For our young players, though, academic education is one of the last things on their minds. There are the exceptions across the country but the majority of our young players aren't academically minded and more often than not, we find that players actually exit secondary education with very little.

This of course needs to change, but in order to generate change we must understand the reasons for a decline in academic performance as players get older.

When entering the world of professional football three years ago, I began to question not the academic side of teaching and learning but the recognition – by schools, clubs and others – of education's role in developing the life skills of young footballers.

Learning for Life

Within football, we can all have a positive influence on the types of life skills we develop in our young players. Life skills such as appropriate behaviour, being a role model, and demonstrating the right attitude, are some of the essential things that we can help produce (more detail on these can be found in chapter 13).

The need for coaches, parents, and teachers to understand the importance of developing the person has never come at a greater time. A recent two-part article in *The Times* highlighted how educational and personal development is 'essential' for players who do not get a scholarship at 16 or a professional contract. The statistics are alarming, to say the least; 96% of scholars signed at 16 will not play again from the age of 18. 98% of players signed as professionals will not be playing by the age of 21.

Even with these statistics staring the football population in the face, it can remain difficult to convince not only young players but parents, coaches and clubs as well, that it is so important to have a Plan B. This 'Plan B', many feel, gets in the way of goal achievement within football. Even though there are some fantastic examples of clubs (both elite and grassroots) that emphasise the importance of education and personal development, we still lag behind in preparing our young players for a life both in and out of football.

Developing essential life skills is not the responsibility of the coach or club alone; parents have the ultimate responsibility to educate their sons and daughters on these attributes. But coaches and clubs should be looking to complement parents when in contact with young players.

What do players need?

At present, we seem to be stuck between a rock and a hard place when it comes to academic education and our young players. In schools, players who are seen to be 'talented' are often given the opportunity to compete for school, county, and clubs regardless of academic performance. Another paragraph from my assignment outlined a potential issue of why we struggle with educating young people:

'It has often been said that if you treat a man like a beast for long enough, you will create one. It is not so different in the context of youth. If you make them feel like nothing in the context of education, make them feel like they cannot achieve, then they will be nothing. And unfortunately that has happened in the past to so many, who have turned out exactly how they were made.

There are, of course, plenty of professional clubs that run excellent day-release programmes for younger players, and provide support during this time; but we must question whether clubs are doing enough across the board to help national development. Not only this but younger players who may not attend release programmes, or players who are not in professional clubs, fail to obtain this type of support and therefore fail to understand how and why life and academic education can benefit them.

Hearing from a number of education professionals involved in football, and academy managers, it has been said that young players can and do suffer from a huge loss of identity if they are not selected for a scholarship in professional academies. Consider how, from around the age of 10, a young person's *identity is football* (especially if they are deemed to be 'talented'). They will play football in school, for their school, for clubs, be seen as a player by others (and not necessarily a 'person'). Accordingly, they will often lose out on some of the essential life skills needed outside the world of football such as dealing with failure, developing mental toughness, or developing sustained self-belief.

Our job here

The previous chapter outlined a number of key areas where clubs, schools and coaches can aid the development and understanding of education. When it comes to developing important life skills there is still more that we can all do though.

The first and most important aspect from a coach's point of view is that players (even young ones) should be seen, and communicated with, as people, not players. The ramifications of creating an environment where we entrap young players in the bubble of football can have damaging effects on football. The importance of talking about key life skills, school and academic work, and behaviour and attitude outside football, should be at the forefront of every coach's mind.

In schools: Even from a very young age (8-9 years old) players will be the subject of attention if they are deemed to have 'talent' in football (or anything else!). It is here that schools (both primary and secondary) must continue to set the same (and if not higher standards) for those individuals. Teaming up with parents and clubs, schools can offer the help required for developing essential life and professional skills expected of a top class performer. For example, if teachers, parents and coaches were to ask a mix of questions (similar to those in the previous chapter) you can begin to build up an understanding of what is required; questions such as:

- *Why* do we go to school?
- *How* can it help you in your life? (Ask for reasons)
- *Can* it help you to become a better player? (If so, how/why? What does it develop?)
- *Could* you use things you learn in football to help in school?

The answers our young players give will vary greatly, which is both to be expected and appreciated (as we are all unique) and we (as coaches) can use this information to mould and develop these players. It can also be used to maintain behavioural standards, to bring players back down to earth. Even in grassroots football, attaching school behaviour and attitude (not grades) can go some way towards encouraging a positive response from young players.

During scholarships: As players get older and enter the latter stages of becoming a professional football player, the main responsibilities fall on the clubs who have the players full time. This means that individuals are exposed to the working world of the football industry and (if not careful) can fall very deeply into its enclosed bubble – forgetting what the real world is really like.

Here, clubs (alongside coaches, education and welfare staff, and teammates) play an essential role in maintaining a check on reality and understanding the difficult demands that are placed on youngsters each day. It is here that many players fall short of the mark and a lot more work should be done to develop the person and not just the player.

For example, after attending a League Football Education (LFE) conference, I learned that some clubs put on community-based work that all scholars must take part in. Some get them involved in coaching the younger groups at the academy (developing skills, being a role model, remembering where they came from). One academy manager in the north of England spoke about getting the boys involved in an initiative that saw them sleeping rough for the night so that they could experience what it was like to be homeless.

It is here, at a time when young players are going through physical, psychological and emotional changes, that ever-increasing workloads/demands are placed on them. It is little wonder that so many fail to achieve their dreams within this two year window so it is of even more importance that coaches, teachers and club management keep up to date and are continually checking on the wellbeing of those young players.

An ever-increasing issue: We commonly see the young 'footballer' take less and less interest in school as they get close to achieving a professional apprenticeship/scholarship. Education here should be seen not as a chore but as a development of themselves and an opportunity to display that they are willing and capable of achieving in all aspects of their lives. If they do not, and choose to demonstrate a poor attitude towards education then that alone is informative when clubs come to deciding on who may receive a professional contract.

So, what skills and education must we encourage our young players to learn? Do we tell them to forget their dreams? Of course not. More often than not we use this concept of education as being their 'plan B'. This to me, however, is incorrect and further emphasises the back seat mentality of education to young players. Instead, education should be seen as a joint venture with football, where professional, academic and personal development can continue within an elite setting. The education of life skills and personal development should continue to be central when it comes to education because it is these qualities (leadership, attitude, behaviour, respect, work rate) that helps young players get to where they want to go.

Summary

Parents, teachers and coaches must decide how we want to teach the youth of today. This involves not just the academic side of education but also necessary life skills and understanding that underpins success and how it can be achieved. Speaking to an U21 development coach recently, I was told that, "players must learn to do what they may hate just as well as what they love. They must treat them with the same dedication, time, and respect as one another". Here then is where life education, for me, flourishes. Remember, good people make good players and what better way to develop good people than by providing essential education to promote this.

11. How we learn

If you are not willing to learn then no one can help you. If you are determined to learn then no one can stop you. Unknown

Football has certainly taken on a more holistic and structured way of developing players in recent years. There is a greater emphasis on things that, even a decade ago, wouldn't have been considered. The realisation that players do not all learn in the same way has promoted new methods of coaching, teaching and instruction to try to give our homegrown players the best opportunity of making it in the professional game.

Seminars, conferences and courses are now geared towards giving the coach as many options as possible that can be transferred onto the training pitch. We are inundated with methods, opinions, and resources, all of which are designed to help. The key question, though, is do we know what we are trying to teach? And within that, do we know how best to put it across?

What is learning?

There is a range of different ways in which we could define learning. The Oxford dictionary defines learning as "the acquisition of knowledge or skills through study, experience or being taught." Many of us in football will describe learning along the lines of getting players to understand the technical, tactical, social and psychological demands of football. Others may simply say that players learn to play the game through understanding their roles and responsibilities on the pitch. However you choose to define learning in football, or in any other area of life, it must be made clear to the person and the player.

A really good football-related activity for your players is to get them into teams and have them write down words they associate with training. For example, see if players understand the terms 'drop', 'press', 'body shape', etc., and talk about them. Look for textbook answers, opinions, and then practical demonstrations from the players to show understanding. You must watch the players learn and discuss how each word/cue can relate to their own learning in football. A big advantage of doing this at the start of the season is that you are telling players that they are going to be learning something. Far too often, coaches assume that players know what they are going to be learning and why they are learning it. Often this can cause confusion. If you have individuals who are afraid of speaking when they do not understand something, then you have already lost them. Introduce players to learning topics, themes and session titles so that players know – from the start – what they are going to be doing.

An activity such as this is important, as you are able to tell the players where learning occurs, why learning is important, and how it can benefit them in all areas of life. Young people have an innate ability to leave 'learning' behind in specific environments (the classroom, the training pitch) when, more often than not, learning straddles a range of environments in their lives.

We often get caught up by teaching and giving advice on what we deem to be 'in our remit'. Obviously, our remits can be wide and varied though. Learning, as defined above, also means giving young people insight and knowledge into our own experiences and world experiences. This is unlimited! Learning needs to be recognised as occurring every day. Young people need to understand that learning occurs all the time.

I often tell my students, in the classroom, that what they learn follows them onto the training pitch. I also highlight that this learning might not be something academic, it could be related to personal development or an understanding and learning of NOT doing something. Far too often, we judge learning on things that can/should be done, learning actually works both ways and understanding not to do something is learning too.

Personal learning must come first

When we talk about learning in society, we often associate it with school and academic qualifications. Many people restrict learning to the classroom environment or say that learning a sport or activity is only done 'when you do it'. This is not true and is an attitude that holds back the development of young footballers. Today's player must demonstrate more than technical ability to make the grade at the top level,

Key fundamentals that are often lacking in young people and players are things that some of us may refer to as:

- A great attitude
- Good philosophy of life
- Old school values

Whatever you may call them, people need certain fundamentals to be successful. It is the fundamentals that often define who people are. Some call it character.

What we would like young people to be… or develop/learn		
Self-Motivation	Enthusiasm	Manners
Being Respectful	Aware (of self and others)	Reflective
Hard Working	Open-Minded	Honest
Creative	Curious	Resilient
Trustworthy	Disciplined	Reliable
The majority of the above are not developments of a footballer or a student, instead they are things we would like a PERSON to develop		

With young players, it is important to avoid stereotyping what learning is. Instead, we need to teach things that have a positive personal benefit to their lives. How many times have we seen, heard or spoken about young players who have bags of potential but their attitude isn't right for the game? Or how often have we come across young players who could be so much better if they listened more, paid attention to detail, and tried even after failure.

How players learn

Many players start their football careers, as 4-5 year olds, being taken by their mum or dad to a new 'little kickers' style coaching company where they play, have fun, get plenty of touches on the ball, and learn basic technical techniques over a period of time. This style of learning is similar for individuals in most domains, whether at work and learning a new job, as coaches building up an armoury of coaching practices, or as a young person first attending school and learning how to read and write. We all start off in the same way, as novices.

We are aware that learning takes time and that is can be broken down into four key stages, which are seen below (image adapted from one in the Intelligently Wired Brain Manual):

The Four Stages of Learning

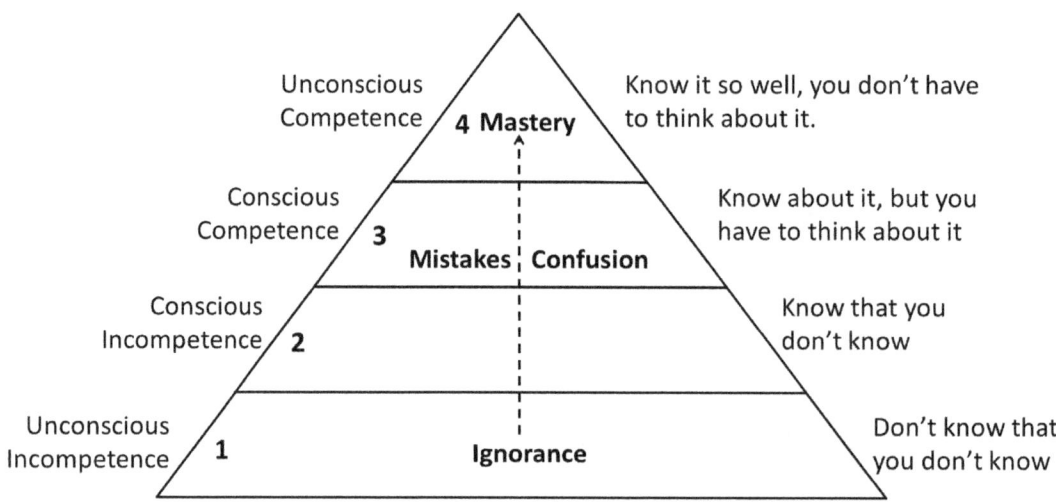

Along the left-hand side of the pyramid is the name of each stage, the right tells us what to expect when we are in each stage. Although mainly utilised in education, this pyramid process is easily transferrable to football. Let's take a look.

First, our 'unconscious incompetence' stage sees our young players attending football practice and not knowing what to do. Coaches introduce them to a ball and get them working on the basics (dribbling, passing, receiving, etc.). In this stage, players should not be overloaded with teaching… young children are already resourceful in how to learn. They watch and observe others (like friends in practice). Here the detail from coaches often comes in the form of demonstration; so we show, and then we let them do.

The second stage sees our young players recognising what they are not good at. This 'conscious incompetence' stage sees players generally being able to do some of the basics but now they want to be able to perform skills such as a stepover or a Cruyff turn. Here coaches take more time to teach their young players by breaking the move down. We often give some technical information as well before letting them head off and have a go. Again, we allow plenty of time for learning to take place and provide some basic verbal cues and advice on how to perform the skill correctly.

As our players grow and progress we often see them in the third stage of learning, known as the 'conscious competence' stage. Here players will be able to do the basics and be able to play in games where principles of play have come into effect. Now their performances are determined by the decisions they make on the pitch. This is what often separates a grassroots player from a young academy player. Technically, they may both be competent but the understanding of the game and being able to deal with problems on the pitch will cause some players to fall short of moving forward. This stage is probably where coaches must have the most influence, using a range of methods to try and support and develop players. There are four traditional styles for coaching/teaching, here.

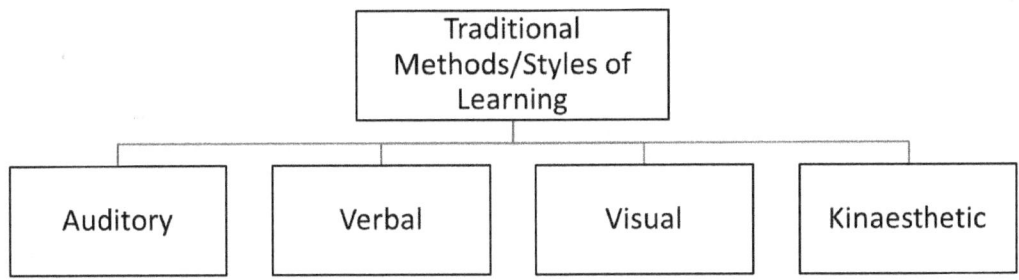

Coaches will try telling, showing, questioning and instructing, and most importantly, they should let players have a go. Here, coaches must consider the number and type of methods used, as too much of one method will often cause learning to plateau. On the flipside, too much variation can often lead to confusion as players lack a consistent way to learn. It is a delicate stage of development and something that many struggle to get right.

Our final stage of 'unconscious competence' sees players performing autonomously. By this, we mean that players are able to perform, problem solve, and make the right decisions without really thinking about it. By this stage, correct decisions have come from both training and game experience, alongside the guidance of coaches and teammates. It is this stage that coaches are looking to get young players to, as quickly as possible. The issue here is that players must have travelled successfully through the first three stages before reaching what can be seen as 'performance mastery' on the pitch.

It is a mistake to think we can skip stages two and three and assume players are capable of moving straight into stage four. This is not the case and time must be taken for development to take place.

How do we know they are learning?

Effectively, it can be difficult to see whether players and people are learning. Generally, in football, we are looking for players to demonstrate the skills, techniques and understanding that we are trying to instil in them during training and games. Coaches often use a short Q&A during a session and get misled into thinking players are learning when they offer some fantastic textbook answers.

When looking for learning in football we know it is about 'walking the walk'. We must see it! But be aware that if you don't see it – that does not mean learning has not occurred. This calls for coaches and others to demonstrate patience with players.

One method of assessing whether players have learned, or not, is through another useful educational approach, known as Bloom's Taxonomy. Having recently been revised to include 'creativity' at the top of its list, Bloom's taxonomy gives a great indication of where someone might be within the learning process. Bloom's taxonomy can be related brilliantly into the learning processes of a young football player (see diagram below, adapted from the one on the Sam Houston State University webpage).

Bloom's Revised Taxonomy

Higher Order Thinking

Creating
Generating new ideas, products or ways of viewing things
Designing, constructing, planning, producing, inventing

Evaluating
Justifying a decision or course of action
Checking, hypothesising, critiquing, experimenting, judging

Analysing
Breaking information into parts to explore understanding and relationships
Comparing, organising, deconstructing, interrogating, finding

Applying
Using information in another familiar situation
Implementing, carrying out, using, executing

Understanding
Explaining ideas or concepts
Interpreting, summarising, paraphrasing, classifying, explaining

Remembering
Recalling Information
Recognising, listing, describing, retrieving, naming, finding

The first three processes of remembering, understanding, and applying can be related to the technical side of the game; we have all seen a young player (between 5-6 years old) actively look up to the sky thinking about how to dribble a football when they first begin, or taking their time when trying to perfect an inside hook turn. What young people and players are trying to do here is understand how a technique is done; then they try to apply that technique. As coaches, we then test whether they have progressed in a particular technique.

In football coaching, we often look for players to reach 'conscious competency' by practicing techniques over and over again. However, at the three higher areas of Bloom's taxonomy (analysing, evaluating, and creating) we are now looking at what has been termed a higher level/order of thinking. This is something that separates the very best players from the good players. This is where we can fail to develop our youngsters on a consistent level. We do not give our players the opportunity to develop the effective game understanding to meet these higher levels of learning.

When working on the three areas (analysing, evaluating and creating) we must relate them to what happens in game situations. I am sure coaches reading this have all said something like this to their players, 'You've seen what they are trying to do, communicate with your teammates and fix it!' Many of us may have at times given them the answer. But in order to achieve a higher level of learning, we must now take the plunge and leave our players alone. Let them work it out for themselves in games (a coach is not needed on a game day except to put the nets up and hand out the kit). If players feel they always have you there to 'bail' them out with an answer they are never going to analyse an issue and then create a solution. It is the development of the top three domains where top coaches earn their money and is something that we must ingrain in them.

Methods of Teaching

There are a wide variety of methods used to help learning take place. One method of teaching is to find the right balance between consistency and variety in your practices. We have some excellent different types of training methods (presented in Chapter 5) that we can use but finding the right balance is key.

A lot of clubs, through EPPP processes, have developed philosophies of play that the club will use as the 'consistency' part, meaning that coaches will look to instil explicit key fundamentals into every player. The variation then comes from the breakdown of the season into weeks and the introduction of defensive, attacking and transitional topics (playing out from the goalkeeper, breaking the lines when possession has been regained, attacking from wide areas, for example). This is something coaches and clubs need to do a lot more of within the grassroots to be able to close the gap between themselves and academy football.

Allowing for trial and error is a common and widely used method of getting players to learn things. Often, coaches can be too hasty in wanting players to get the basics right. What we must understand is that, with our sessions, we are not providing the opportunity to get things correct; we are simply providing the opportunity for players to *try* things. If everyone got everything right all the time the world would be a much better place, that's for sure! So recognise when a player just needs that time to test something out (such as a particular skill or making the correct decision).

Positive reinforcement is an important method for facilitating learning! Praising what a player may be doing right can help build confidence and give that player the freedom and belief to try something new. With reinforcement, do not just congratulate a player on doing something well, but instead tell the player *why* you are congratulating them. Helping the player understand *what* they did well, *how* they did it, and *why* it benefits their performance can be far more rewarding and educational than a simple 'well done'.

Following on, players will begin to take more risks in trying new things; their decision-making skills are likely to be tested here and the guidance of coaches is the next step in developing a young player. Guiding players and facilitating what they do means one very important thing – don't give the player an answer, there are no correct answers in football – there are only opinions on how a player or team should play.

Instead, look to 'sell' an idea on how things could be done but give the player room to improvise and come to their own conclusions. By telling players what we want, we can sometimes take away some of the decision making that we associate with higher-level thinking (which is what is needed at the top level). This is not to say coaches can't always tell a player what they want, but be aware that too much may simply stifle an individual's creativity and turn them into a one-dimensional player.

There are, of course, a range of methods that can be used to help develop players; what we must consider is how our players learn, identify at what stage(s) of learning they reside, and which processes they are currently going through. By analysing this, we can begin to help players learn what they are doing in a variety of positive ways.

Summary

The biggest obstacle we face in creating and developing excellent young football players is not always down to what we do on the pitch. How children learn and our understanding of what needs to be done to improve the individual has a huge effect on whether young players will grow up and develop into top international players. Understanding the stages and the processes of learning that must take place is important for coaches, teachers and parents to know. It allows for patience in key areas in a young player's life. We must identify what needs to be done to take them to the next level – when they are ready – in order to develop the footballer and the person as well.

12. Must nurture; Do not leave it to nature

We are what we repeatedly do. Excellence, therefore, is not an act, but a habit. Aristotle

The nature vs. nurture debate causes great division, especially within the Psychology community. Without delving into too much social science, this chapter looks at the need to nurture young players to improve them, and also help them become better people.

What happens if we leave development down to nature?

We cannot escape the simple fact that nature has a key role to play in our development; we are often governed, as people, by various traits and characteristics that we have inherited from our parents. Those traits will have an underlying influence on what we do as people, as much as players.

However, nature alone does not determine development or success. Take an example of a young player who comes to you and whose mum or dad is an ex-international player. We often automatically assume that the child will be a good player. However, although the child will have a genetic makeup that many may see as having potential or talent (discussed in chapter 8) this does not predict whether he/she will be a good player themselves.

Nature is often seen as the driver of footballing success. Is a player naturally talented? Does a player naturally have the right mindset? In turn, we often use nature as an excuse for a player *not* showing talent or developing well enough.

What is essential for the development of young players and people in this country is that we do not leave people by the wayside under the assumption that nature has not blessed them with the traits to be successful. Doing this automatically narrows our field of progression and willingness to work with others! Nature is by no means an enemy, it is essential as it helps make 'us who we are'; however, what must be recognised is the link and interaction nature has with the concept of 'nurturing' and how much more of an effect we can have through doing it the right way.

Why is nurturing so important?

The Oxford Dictionary defines nurturing as "to care for and protect (something or someone) while they are growing". A fitting definition for coaches to recognise when developing young players, no doubt. Nurturing is based around the need to help, encourage, guide and cherish individuals to become better players and people.

The right types of environments can have a huge influence on the development of young players (and is something that a lot of clubs have taken on board in recent times). Of course, by the time most young players actually arrive at a club (grassroots or academy) they have already been nurtured by numerous people including parents, families and close friends.

The nurturing of a young person's 'psychological core', where attitudes, beliefs and values are shaped, often relates directly from the type of interaction parents and families have with their young children. The importance of nurturing is not restricted to the emotional development of the person either; parents and families who actively encourage their children to 'play' and be active are aiding physical development, whilst nutrition (and the right type of nutrition, in particular) is also relevant.

This chapter is not here to tell anyone how best to raise children. We each have our own views, methods and ideas of how to do this and no one way works best for all. What should be considered, instead, is the interaction between the key environments we expose our children to. Often, football is only concerned with developing the player, and clubs create cultures that revolve around the EPPP format, encouraging topics and learning objectives to be seen, used, and reflected upon. In turn, we talk about the four-corner model in football (technical, tactical, physical, and psychosocial) and gear our sessions around what we feel is the development of all four. Realistically all four are only (and in some cases rightly) geared towards football. It is very difficult for coaches to go beyond this framework but it is something they need to do.

What can we do better?

Nurturing our young players into becoming well-rounded young people requires us to do a range of things better than we currently are. It is about instilling the right types of habits in individuals across a wide range of situations and environments; behaviours that carry across school, football, being out with friends, and spending time with family, for example. Rather than differences within these environments – consistency is key!

Barcelona's famous 'La Masia' is the home of their youth team. A place that has turned out a range of homegrown stars that have graced the world stage. Yet look at a standard timetable for the young players within the Barcelona ranks… there is normally only an hour and forty-five minutes worth of football a day!

La Masia Director, Carles Folguera, has stated that the club wants intellectual players, and that physicality is not important. He has also described the importance of education for those who may not make it, or those who want to pursue other careers. Even an academy that is renowned for producing world-class youngsters still has a Plan B for their players at the forefront of its thinking.

Daily schedule of La Masia student

06:45 Get up and make bed

07:00 Breakfast at La Masia

07:30 School bus pick-up

08:00-14:00 School

14:15 Lunch

15:00 Free hour

16:00-18:00 Added schooling

19:00-20:45 Training

21:00 Shower/Bus back to La Masia

21:30 Dinner

22:00 TV/Internet

(Taken from the BBC Report in February 2011, entitled – The house that built Barca)

The strength here comes from the realisation that in order to develop top players you must embed a culture that promotes excellence through a person's life. Note that players have to make their own beds, for example. Football, education and a creative and development-orientated environment is essential to success.

Now obviously we are not all at Barcelona, with their facilities or resources; we may be a simple but passionate chartered grassroots club in the Midlands, South East or the North West of England, but that doesn't mean we cannot instil good habits and create development-orientated environments within our own club.

Below I have listed some basic ideas that clubs (academies, grassroots, whomever!) can look to introduce to build a nurturing environment.

Idea 1 – Have all coaches take 5 minutes at the beginning of training (during the introductory activity, for example) to ask each player to name one thing they learnt in school that day. If possible, refer back to football (for example if a student tells you something to do with geography, have them try to name players from five different countries).

Idea 2 – As a coach ask your players at the end of the session to thank whoever brought them to your session that night (mum, dad, family friend, brother, sister, whoever!) and ask them *why* we need to thank them. Try to get across to the players the concept of love and appreciation. You can always get your players to scream a big 'thank you for bringing me' at the end (you'll often find this rejuvenates a lot of parents too) to strengthen bonds with family and friends.

Idea 3 – Discuss a player's school behaviour and work ethic in school with parents, and relate this to their football. Try to stay clear of attaching successful behaviour to good grades because a child can try really hard and not live up to others' expectations (and that's okay). Having a relationship between parents and coaches/clubs will reinforce good habits, behaviours and values – and show a unity to the player who is then more likely to find a consistency in their behaviour.

Idea 4 – Have clubs create and run education and football fun days. This is something that local clubs, especially, can accomplish by liaising with schools. For example, put on a maths workshop by looking at basic stats in football (percentages in possession), PE linked to fitness needed for football, food technology linked to a good footballer's diet, language lessons teaching kids basic calls, and more.

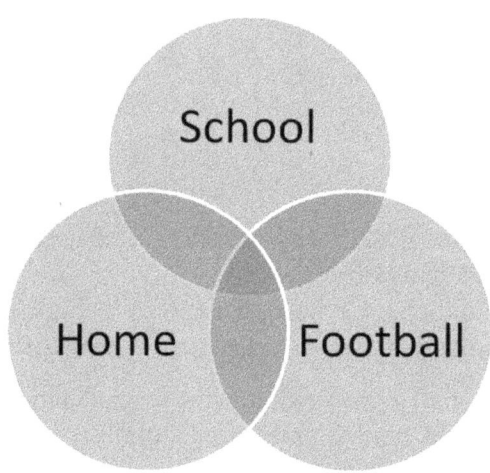

Now, of course, not all these ideas will work. Accept that there will always be that parent who is never happy, or unwilling to mix and mingle; that coach who will scream, shout and want to win at all costs; and a club that may not be overly helpful. But, overall, if you begin to put things in place that facilitate a nurturing environment, and develop good behavioural, intellectual and social habits, then you are going to get a well-developed person at the end of it.

What can professional clubs and governing bodies do even better?

As well as the ideas highlighted above, professional clubs have the resources and personnel to go one step further in certain areas. For example, club-appointed welfare and education officers should be making themselves available to all players and parents. They should liaise with, and go into, schools to discuss a person's progress. By encouraging parents to liaise with club personnel and schools there should be a far more interactive and consistent approach visible to the youngster. In turn, performance reports (school reports) can be exchanged, grades checked and monitored (and support can be given where needed) and feedback shared.

The Football Association can also follow suit. The introduction of F.A. Mentors could potentially be a great idea in terms of educating coaches, but what must be understood is that, more often than not, the coaching side of football is not the highest developmental priority. Instead, personal development in coaches is of far greater importance, especially at grassroots level where we need to tackle winning vs. development, parental influences, lack of resources, and understanding the personal development of our players. These areas need to be at the forefront of an F.A. Mentor's role, not simply telling coaches what type of practice to put on.

Summary

Nurturing young players has a huge impact on their development, both as footballers and people. Leaving development to nature has its downfalls and a lot more should (and could) be done by coaches to promote nurturing environments where players come to learn. Here it is the responsibility of clubs (both grassroots and elite) to encourage and devise methods that bring in a range of positive influences and reinforcements to benefit young players and help them become better.

13. Having a core set of beliefs and values

The difference between a successful person and others is not a lack of strength, not lack of knowledge, but rather a lack of will. Vince Lombardi

Core values and beliefs represent an area that young people need to recognise. It is important that we introduce our values and beliefs and tell players *why* we believe in them. In turn, it is imperative that we ultimately allow players to make their own choices.

Development of Values

The following values are in no particular order of preference or ranking. Each of these values, I believe, leads to success, with success being satisfaction, fulfilment and happiness - not the traditional view of medals, trophies and titles. My own values, beliefs, and what I deem to be success, are unique to me. Others will learn, accept, reject and develop their own set, so always be prepared to listen to them when discussing this topic.

Value 1 - Having a high work ethic

What is work ethic?

Work ethic can be seen as the ability to work hard across a range of situations, demonstrating reliability, respect and value to the job on a consistent basis.

Why is it needed?

Within football, the practical application of work ethic and work rate is demonstrated through physical actions that show a desire to cover distance at a high intensity. This is commonly a prerequisite for clubs. Clubs want players to demonstrate high work ethics in training as much as matches in order to develop physically, technically and tactically.

Work ethic can also come in other forms such as education and personal development. Here a work ethic translates to a willingness and desire to work on, and develop, key skills that could benefit players over the long term, preventing short term emotion (such as boredom, unwillingness or laziness) from inhibiting development.

How do we instil a work ethic in young players?

Method 1 – Positively reinforce the 'process' rather than the 'outcome'

Here it is essential for coaches to praise the process (the actions that occur before a positive outcome has been demonstrated, such as scoring a goal) behind a player's development and not the outcome. So, praising effort and application or work rate and highlighting where the rewards are seen when hard work is demonstrated is huge for the technical and personal development of a young player.

Method 2 – Providing examples of positive role models

Here coaches, parents and teachers can make the most of technology by providing links to videos, interviews, and articles from a range of sports that focus on work ethic and working hard. Players can be sent links (perhaps one every 3-4 weeks depending on the age of players) and asked to read chosen articles before providing their own feedback. By showing examples of what a high work ethic provides, players may respond by trying to incorporate this positive habit.

Value 2 - Developing Mental Toughness

What is Mental Toughness?

Mental toughness is having an attitude or mindset that allows a player to persevere with a task despite experiencing failure (once or on a number of occasions) and not losing the desire, confidence or motivation to achieve in the future.

Why is it needed?

Being able to persevere despite failure is essential in football as players will often experience failure. They will make mistakes in training and in games, will be affected by team selection, club transfers, and the renewal of contracts to name but a few.

Players are expected to demonstrate mental toughness across a wide range of environments, such as education, at home and in social situations. Players coming through the youth ranks are exposed to so many pressures and expectations that a mentally tough attitude and approach is almost essential.

How can we instil mental toughness in our players?

Method 1 – Educate players on the 'intention' of an action

Coaches have an incredibly important job when it comes to developing mental toughness as we think of it as occurring after failure. Here coaches need to ask the player what the intention was behind a particular action that may not have worked. They can then begin to give constructive feedback and options for how players can improve and succeed and explain how failure is just another path for learning something new. If you can educate a player to understand that as long as they have an intended action they want to carry out – then it is just about developing that action.

Method 2 – Carry out a 'Home Team Ref' session

Coaches can put on a range of sessions, including a 'home team ref' session, where a small part of the session (in an SSG for example) can be created with the majority of the decisions given to one team. We then get players used to controlling their emotions and understanding where, why and how something may be affecting them. Mental toughness may mean controlling emotions and sticking to a game plan.

Value 3 - Respect (for oneself and others)

What is Respect?

Respect is the understanding and appreciation a person has for another person based on their past experience, knowledge and position. Introducing people to the concept of respect as early as possible in a range of different environments is desirable.

Why is it needed?

Obviously, you are never going to enjoy everyone's company within a team but holding respect for your teammates and staff, and supporting them in training and during games creates cohesion. Teammates that do not respect one another will not want to work hard for one another and collective motivation and confidence will not be present.

How do we instil respect in our players?

Method 1 – Handshakes before and after training games

Here coaches can have players shake the coach's and teammates' hands. It is a good idea to explain what shaking hands means (in terms of respect). Players should do this in training and games.

Method 2 – Developing a positive posture when in training and games

Coaches can encourage and show players how to maintain a positive posture when talking and interacting with coaching staff and other players. Standing up straight (no slouching) with hands behind the back and eyes focused on whoever is talking develops respect and the understanding to take on what is being said/asked. This does not mean a strict military stance must be demonstrated everywhere, but within team talks, especially, body language should be positive and respectful.

Value 4 - Honesty

What is Honesty?

Honesty is about being truthful in your opinions and actions. It is about expressing what is morally right whether it benefits you or not.

Why is it needed?

Teaching our young players the value of honesty is a huge step in their personal as well as professional development. Teaching young players to be honest with themselves can allow you as a coach, teacher or parent to integrate other values around it; for example, if a player was late for training and upon reflection was honest in admitting that they set off later than they should have, then we can educate players on the importance of being disciplined and organised to ensure it doesn't happen in the future. Players that are dishonest and give excuses, blame others and circumstances will find it more difficult to embed better values into their lives, which could impact upon their development.

An honest player who first reflects on their own attitude is more likely to be open to guidance, willing to work on weaknesses, and not make excuses when things don't go their way.

How do we instil honesty in our players?

Method 1 – Reward honesty, Educate on dishonesty

Creating an environment where honesty is rewarded is massive as one honest act can kick-start a chain of events that promotes and sustains honesty through a season and beyond. Coaches may start players who have demonstrated honesty, whether that appears in work rate, or speaking up about mistakes and attributing them to something they need to work on. If you play honest players who are willing to work hard and do the right things, that can have a positive effect on others.

Coaches then have the responsibility to educate those who lie, and be supportive and constructive with them, while at the same time being firm on the punishments and perceptions players create if they do lie. Here a coach may substitute a player who has dived, explaining the reasoning behind why they were brought off and that it will not be tolerated. Also, it gives the coach the opportunity to explain to the player the perception they create of themselves (a dishonest player) and that it is a form of cheating to gain an unfair advantage.

Note – consider showing players the clip of Aaron Hunt (Werder Bremen) telling the referee that he dived and not to award the penalty originally given by the match official.

Method 2 – Focus Group Sessions

A great idea for older age groups (14+) is to hold termly focus groups where coach and players sit round a table and have an honest conversation. Here, areas such as training sessions, player performances, attitude, and behaviour can all be addressed in a team setting and goals created to move forward. This can be a difficult thing to get right as young people may not understand the concept of 'what is said in a focus group stays in a focus group' and may use it outside to insult or aggravate. However, if you can manage and educate players on recognising that honesty in the form of constructive feedback can benefit development, then this can be a very powerful tool.

Value 5 - Self-Discipline

What is Self-Discipline?

Self-discipline relates to a number of key qualities such as resilience, patience, and the self-control that maintains a set of standards and behaviours.

Why is it needed?

Self-discipline is an essential value that young players must look to instil; many core values branch off from it. For example, being disciplined may affect how organised a players is (a player could make sure that his/her kit is ready the day before training). Time management could also be built into self-discipline with players looking to ensure they are at training 10-15 minutes before it starts. Without self-discipline, effort may diminish in training and games, preparation becomes non-existent, and a willingness to learn and improve is less likely to occur.

How do we instil self-discipline in our players?

Method 1 – Having players set a game day alarm

Although developing self-discipline can fall into a large range of other values (such as taking responsibility), one specific method can involve a player setting their own alarm clock. This can be done using their phones or by getting them a little alarm clock and telling them to set it to a time which they feel is suitable for waking up, getting ready, eating a good breakfast, and getting to the game.

Method 2 – Writing up a weekly to do list for football

Developing on from the above method (used as a starting point for younger players), players can devise a weekly 'to do' list where they write down all the things they need to have done in preparation for games and training.

This could include things such as cleaning boots, having shin pads and kit ready for each session, preparing drinks bottles and snacks, etc. By putting players in charge, you are giving them more responsibility to be disciplined if they want to train and play football every week.

Value 6 - Taking Responsibility

What is Responsibility?

Taking responsibility means being accountable for your own actions, first and foremost, and not placing blame on other people, the environment or circumstances.

Why is it needed?

Responsibility is an important value to instil because it enables players to reflect and act on their own thinking, actions, and intuition. This leads to independent thinkers who will look to problem solve in a range of different ways; coaches are there to help guide and offer support when it is needed.

Creating players that take responsibility means that leaders are developed, communication is improved, and ownership and accountability are at the forefront of the player's learning.

How do we develop responsibility in our players?

Method 1 – Change of Captains/Vice Captains

One of the best ways to introduce responsibility in young footballers is to give the responsibility of being a captain to everyone. Each week you allocate a player to be captain for one week in both training and a game. They will be in charge of things such as: organising teams, meeting the officials, collecting feedback on performances from the team to present to coaches, and making sure all equipment is in and presentable.

Method 2 – Player tasks

A big area of developing responsibility is through sharing it out. This can come in the form of handing out different tasks (e.g. carrying water bottles, setting up pitches, collecting kit, etc.). This can work on a rotating basis with the coach assigning responsibilities to players every few months.

Value 7 - Humility

What is Humility?

Humility is about teaching young people the importance of being humble about their achievements and not belittling anyone who may not have achieved in the same way. Being modest about achievements means a person still recognises the need for improvement.

Why is it needed?

With increased performance, players will become more confident and it is essential they know the difference between confidence and arrogance. Arrogance is not always bad as long as young players recognise that in order to perform consistently, to the highest level expected, they must train hard consistently and want to learn.

Everyone should be excited and proud of their achievements but developing and teaching a greater understanding of being humble about one's own ability is likely to keep you grounded and ensure that you always train to be better (train like a contender, play like a champion).

How do we develop humility in our players?

Method 1 – Develop an Empathy corner in sessions

A great way to develop humility within players is by educating them to understand that success cannot always be achieved. This can be demonstrated in an 'empathy corner' within a session. This involves taking 10 minutes of a session to go through what mistakes were made and why they were made, whether it was down to a technical mistake, a breakdown in communication or something else. Here we are trying to express to players that mistakes happen and, when they do, it's okay, and that we treat mistakes with respect and look for a solution so that when we are successful, we understand what it took to get there (understanding the process of success).

Players can be told that not everyone will succeed at the same pace, or in the same ways, and that being humble about what you learnt is a process that we all go through. Subsequently, a trust and appreciation for what others do will begin to emerge.

Method 2 – Showing evidence of humility in other sports

With older groups, players can be shown humility from outside football. Take J.J. Watt or Michael Jordan and their stories and what it took to get to where they were/are now. Providing this outlook from athletes in the elite phase of their careers, speaking about humility and effort, can help develop an understanding of how success does not appear naturally and how it should not be taken for granted.

Value 8 - Self-belief

What is Self-Belief?

Self-belief is having confidence in oneself, and one's ability, to succeed in a task.

Why is it needed?

Self-confidence is an essential part of development. People who lack self-belief become disengaged, disruptive, aggressive, and lazy, none of which benefits personal development. Often, young players have self-belief up to the point when they experience their first real failure.

Coaches, teachers and parents need to educate young players to understand that failure is only permanent if you stop trying and that youngsters need to have belief in their ability to find a new way around a problem.

How do we instil self-belief in our players?

Method 1 – Create a 'WOW' list for a player

Creating mini WOW lists for players can be an excellent way to help boost their self-belief. Print (and maybe laminate) player sheets upon which three things are listed that a player has done well in training (over a one-week period) or in a game. This can be handed to the player to reflect upon over the weekend and should be brought back to training ready for more positive feedback to be added. WOW lists provide nice visual reinforcement that players can read and even show their parents.

Method 2 – Player to player reviews

Positive encouragement and words from a peer can, at times, have a much greater impact than from a coach. Here, a coach could allocate 15 minutes every 2-4 weeks for players to pair up and write down the things they feel their partner does well and present it to the group. This opens up communication between players and has players recognise that they contribute to the group from the view of their teammates.

Value 9 - Consistency

What is Consistency?

Consistency is the ability to maintain the same set of standards and behaviours across a wide range of environments and situations.

Consistency may fall into *always* being motivated and passionate, or having reliable self-discipline and being honest at all times. Consistency develops good habits, and good habits help drive development and progression.

Here we must be aware that in order to create consistent players and people we have to actively demonstrate our own consistency in what we do. For some, this can be a stumbling block because, as adults, we often display inconsistencies and then fall back on 'do as I say and not as I do'. (Hey, I have done it! We all have!). We must work hard to be consistent as much as our players.

How do we instil consistency in our players?

Method 1 – Develop a routine for training and games

Encourage young players to have a set routine in preparation for training. This might involve players making sure (meticulously) that they have all their kit ready.

Method 2 – Handing over responsibility (linked to responsibility)

Again, coaches and parents can go some way to developing consistency in young players by handing over a set amount of responsibility for certain actions (e.g. washing own boots, bringing a piece of kit/equipment to a game, leading a warm up/starter activity for training or before a game). By handing over responsibility on a regular basis, young players will become consistent with what is expected of them and will develop natural ideas and solutions to problems that they face.

Note – what is extremely important here is that if a player was to forget something or get something wrong, a coach, parent, teacher must ensure that feedback is constructive, offering ideas and examples and not criticism. Remember, we are developing consistency so expect some inconsistencies to occur!

Summary

Positive values and beliefs need to be put across, and developed, in young players and people. You must help players understand why you selected the values you choose to instil by explaining what you feel they can give people. Importantly, not all values and beliefs are going to be shared by everyone, and you must be okay with that. Having a set of core values must be seen by all (coaches, parents, and teachers) as a fundamental building block that drives success and progression. These values and beliefs are what steer us and keep us on track when situations may cause us to lose our way. Develop a set of values that you believe works best for you and your players but enable them to develop their own for their futures.

14. Instilling Confidence

Confidence comes from not always being right but from not fearing to be wrong.
Peter T. McIntyre

Confidence plays a key role in a young person's life. It is what makes a young person put their hand up to go first in a penalty shootout; it is what makes them raise their hand to answer a question in the classroom; it is what gives them the courage to ask out someone they may like.

We often use the term confidence in training, in games, during a team talk, or after a game, to help instil belief in players. However, the term gets batted around so much that it loses meaning as to what confidence is, and what it means to be confident. We must ensure that as coaches, teachers, and parents, we are aware of what confidence really is and how we can develop it.

What is confidence?

Many people talk about confidence but very few understand the constructs of confidence. People who are seen to be confident demonstrate belief in their ability to perform; they are capable of meeting the demands set out in front of them. In football, a player may be confident that they can beat their man in a 1v1 situation, or when in front of goal are confident they are going to score. The major issue with seeing this type of confidence is that it is *not* conducive to long term development and success.

We often see confidence as a particular 'state' which, by definition, is short term. States are ever-changing. What we need to be looking for is a consistent level of confidence in ability across a young player's life, which is often referred to as trait confidence. This trait confidence comes from demonstrating confidence across a wide range of environments and situations (not just football) and this is what we need to develop in our young players.

Developing trait confidence that becomes part of a young person's personality is one of the biggest factors in achieving success. Here we are looking for young players to have confidence in whatever they are doing. Many players have different levels of confidence in different situations. Some will excel in school so will be confident and others will not. Some will have a nurturing and expressive home life that builds confidence, again, others will not.

What trait confidence also brings about is a sense of control for the person, recognising that they are in charge of how they train and play; they understand that 'their best' means doing what they know they can do. This gives players a sense of ownership and responsibility.

What we often do to destroy it

As powerful and wonderful as confidence can be, for young players it is probably the most fragile aspect of their entire development. It can be created and destroyed in the same sentence by others and that can have a long-lasting and damaging effect on the individual. The other main issue with confidence is that even if we are not the ones responsible for damaging it, we may well be the ones who have to deal with a lack of it.

Coaches have a duty, no matter what level they are coaching at, to be positive with their players. Positivity within sessions has an impact because players will recognise that they are able to get things wrong and still be in the coach's good books.

The traditional methods of shouting and yelling at players should be banished.

Yet even now, I see coaches from all levels shout, yell and scream at their players often in relation to a mistake that has been made. When asked for the reason behind an outburst, the coach frequently answers 'They need to recognise what they are doing wrong' or 'They need to learn what to do in those situations', as though shouting and screaming will do that.

Young people will often associate loud voices with negative emotions and reactions due to previous experiences in their life. Think about it, in school when you misbehave, you get shouted at. When you are on the computer way too long at home, your mum will come in and shout at you to get off the computer and go outside. More often than not, the action of shouting is attributed to a negative event and even if shouting occurs in a completely different area of life, young people will associate that negative experience with the situation and react in the same way. They will shut down.

Speaking to a range of full time football scholars, I asked what annoyed them the most about being shouted at, to which the following was said (paraphrased):

'When we get shouted at, it's like they are repeating what we already know. At this level, we know we have done something wrong and we don't need reminding of it. Instead it would be more helpful to let us know, calmly, what to do or tell us it is ok and to try something different.'

What we are seeing here is what I often term 'criticism with construction'. Certainly at the elite youth level many players are primed and prepared to receive a certain amount of criticism and will take it happily if they know that there is going to be reasoning behind it and a plan of what they can do to make it better. When it is not presented in this way, a player's confidence is affected and they will revert back to previous negative states and shut down. Negative states are not confident states.

A lot of confidence destruction (certainly at grassroots level) comes from the pressure to get a result. Although I have seen grassroots teams encouraged to play, there are still way too many clubs that focus on winning; confidence therefore becomes inextricably linked to the result of games. This focus on the win/loss column applies additional pressure on players because they have not yet developed the necessary skills to deal with stress and pressure. If the need to get a result is coupled with shouting and yelling from the sidelines (from coaches and families) then you are going to create and develop low trait confidence in players.

What we need to do to create and build it

Enough of destroying confidence; let's talk about what things we can do to build confidence.

There are a range of different methods coaches use to promote and build confidence in young players but what must be recognised and appreciated is that confidence doesn't always mean rewarding the right things (i.e. you don't need to give out a man of the match award, or a trophy). Sometimes, it is about having players reflect on their achievements and have *them* recognise what they did to get them to that desired outcome.

Don't get me wrong, we all love praise! Often referred to as positive reinforcement, a 'Well done' or 'That was amazing' can lift the spirits of a young player tenfold. The key here is that if we are going to be giving praise as coaches we need to understand that it isn't enough to say 'well done', we need to tell players *why* we are congratulating and praising them. If we, as coaches, can offer constructive praise from an early age, players will then be more likely to understand that the process of *what* and *how* they perform creates the success they wish to feel.

Building confidence is related to developing resilience, and about banishing a fear of failure mentality, which often plagues young players. So recognise what players do well and congratulate them on it. For example *'Well done James, the weight on that pass meant the ball went through to the striker for him to finish'* or *'Alice, that tackle was brilliant because you were able to influence and dominate your opponent with an effective body shape to allow you to put the challenge in at the correct time'*. Specificity is key here; it has far more impact on a young player's development than *'Good job Danny'*.

A simple technique to start off feedback is the use of a question. 'Today you performed brilliantly, and can anyone tell me why?' Players subsequently have the opportunity to highlight why they may feel they have performed well individually, within a unit and as a team. They can even write down any good points and coaches can look to delve a little deeper, making use of effective Q&A to develop deeper analytical thinking. This technique (although time-consuming at times) not only builds confidence but gets players to think a lot more about the reasons behind their performance.

It is important that specific reinforcement is part of a 'performance-orientated environment', where success isn't defined by the result.

Regrettably, in current society, the outcome is always seen as the defining feature of an act. One football match or one grade is deemed to define who a person is. We need young people to understand that focusing on the performance will have a far greater impact than simply focusing on the outcome. Coaches, teachers, and parents need to advocate that one outcome does not define you; one result does not tell people who you are. Instead, breaking performance down into manageable chunks, to tweak, to adjust and to change, will impact far more on overall success in the future.

Take the example of a performance-orientated approach with Alice -

'Alice, when in possession I would like you to try to pass with both feet, when you can, to keep possession for your team in the middle third.'

There is nothing on the outcome of the game, nothing on the performance of anyone else, just a performance objective that she can gauge the success of. And if Alice feels successful, she will grow in confidence.

Building trait confidence comes from recognising the smallest successes in everything a player does, and building on them no matter how small. Celebrate the successes and you will grow confidence that leads players to work harder and smarter for you, and try new things without fear.

Summary

Confidence in a young person's life is essential if they are going to be happy. Confidence is often misunderstood and used alongside terms such as 'winning' and 'reward'.

Developing performance-orientated trait confidence will be far more rewarding and useful for a person in later life as they learn the reasons behind success and accept that confidence and success don't always derive from winning. Developing this type of trait confidence can aid in the development of more positive attributes, such as motivation, determination, and reduce any fear of failure at the same time. Small successes should never be underestimated or neglected because of the way we choose to measure success; others will value smaller steps so understand the smallest of developments and use them as building blocks to progress.

15. Motivation – An Environment Built Around Players

Success seems to be connected with action. Successful people keep moving. They make mistakes, but they don't quit. Conrad Hilton

We would like to think that we are all motivated to do well, be the best, progress and develop in all aspects of our lives. Like confidence, we talk about motivation in football today and assume young players are aware of what it means to be motivated, and what they can do to build motivation in order to progress. Motivation can, in fact, be very complex due to the nature of what each individual wants to achieve. More often than not, we do not share all the same motivations.

What is Motivation?

We can look at motivation as the thing that gives us the drive and direction to go and achieve what we want. For some of us, that is developing players to play in the top flight of English football. For others it might be to achieve an A* in English Literature. In turn, a mother and father might be motivated to provide food and shelter for their young baby girl. Whatever the goal that needs to be 'achieved' we find ourselves motivated by the discrepancy between what we currently have and what we want in the future.

It would be wrong to say that we are all motivated all of the time though. At times, we lack the energy or impetus to go and improve what we currently have. And at times that is completely natural; we must accept that motivation will sometimes diminish due to a range of variables at home, in school, and with friends, as well as in football. It is important for coaches to recognise de-motivation and remind young players why they play the game. The first answer should always be because they love the game (and it's fun!). Players should also recognise that if they want to get better then they must recognise their drop in motivation and seek ways to improve it.

What motivates us?

The table below demonstrates the very simple, but understandable, changes people go through in terms of footballing motivation. It shows how hopes and dreams turn into calculated measured goals that will hopefully lead towards success in the future. As someone progresses through the stages (they are often linked to age and footballing progression) their motivation changes and adapts (and, in all honesty, not always for the better).

Motivational Outlook	What we may see	What they might say
Just play, it's fun	Young kids running, playing, laughing, building social groups.	'I LOVE FOOTBALL' 'I want to play it every day!'
Dream Job	Kids playing for schools and grassroots teams, loving the game and wanting to be their favourite player	'Did you see me do the Ronaldo skill?' 'I'm Aguero! I play like him!'
Would be amazing to be a footballer	Getting slightly older, still with the desire to be the best player in the world because of how amazing players are on television	'Ok, I'll be in defence because I can stop them scoring and you go upfront so we can score goals'
Genuine Opportunity	Could now be in an academy and recognises the chance to play with great players.	'Yeah I play for X academy, we are really good'
Measured goals towards being successful	Older years of adolescence; beginning to recognise the clear and distinct opportunity in front of them. Tries to create environment to succeed.	'Coach, what more do I need to do in order to get more minutes on the pitch?'

Motivation changes as players age and progress. By the time young players are getting to U14's, especially in academies, they are already thinking of getting a full time scholarship! It should be noted that clubs, coaches and parents often have far more input at this stage, make their player/son/daughter aware of the importance of a scholarship far too early, and therefore change the type of motivation felt.

Motivation, as discussed in the previous chapter, is driven by intrinsic and extrinsic rewards.

Whether the motivation is intrinsic or extrinsic – however it draws you or your players in, use it to the best of your ability. Research suggests that being intrinsically motivated presents a better chance of being successful in the long term as you are motivated by personal mastery of a task and that, consequently, motivation levels will remain high even in the face of failure. Compare that to extrinsically motivated individuals who are more likely to remove themselves from difficult tasks in order to avoid failure. If a young player is motivated to be rich and have nice cars then that's fine. Who doesn't want a nice car?

What must be made clear, however, to young players (as well as coaches and parents) is that whether intrinsically or extrinsically motivated – the important aspect lies in the understanding of what it takes to achieve one's goals. Having a full and in-depth understanding, first and foremost, is pivotal because many players become lost and confused with regards to what it takes to be a success and what truly motivates them.

Take this example: when working with my community group (who are aged between 16 and 19 years old) in a sport psychology lesson on motivation, I asked the guys and girls what they are motivated by. Some said money (well, lots said money) some said fame, big house, nice car, etc., the usual. I wrote these down on the white board and drew a dividing line down the middle, with the title 'Things I want' above the things shouted out by the kids. In the column next to it, I wrote the title 'Things I have to do to get the things I want' and tasked the students to write down what they felt they had to do to be successful. This table ended up looking something like this:

Things I want	Things I have to do to get what I want
Money	Work hard
Nice House	Train hard
Fancy Car	Go to sleep early
Fame	Complete homework
Lots of holidays	Go to university

I did the same with an U18 academy side... here is what they put down:

Things I want	Things I have to do to get what I want
Money	Work hard
Nice House	Train hard
Play in the Champions League	Go to sleep early
Represent my country	Eat right

What was most striking to me was not that the left hand column was similar... as everyone knows we pretty much all want the same things. No, what I found to be an issue was that there was very little elaboration on the 'train hard' concept. Talking to these academy players I realised that there had been no real education on 'what' they needed to actually do. There was no breakdown, no goals of what they should be looking to achieve, and how they were going to do it.

How does Motivation affect young players?

Just like anybody else, young football players will go through a rollercoaster of emotions as they try to improve and progress towards the professional game. Factors discussed in this book (education, coaching, and the development of values) will all have an impact on motivation and young players will respond differently to each of them.

We can often recall the positive and negative effects of motivation or the lack of it. We have all, I am sure, at some point had the talk with a young player about how it affects us. The table below shows us some positive and negative factors linked to motivation:

High levels of Motivation	Low levels of Motivation
Increase in confidence and self esteem	Causes anxiety in more stressful situations
More desire to achieve in the face of failure	Causes fear
Perseveres with difficult tasks	Higher dropout rate of tasks and opportunities presented to the player
Develops work ethic	Develops lazy attitude

The obvious way to have an impact on progression and development is by keeping the motivation levels of players high by providing suitable feedback during sessions, positively reinforcing what they do right, and constructively breaking down what they may not be doing well currently.

It is important to give players a path to follow in order to help maintain their motivation. It is equally important to recognise that should clear, precise and relative conversations, demonstrations, and paths come to a standstill, then young players will find themselves at a loose end and will struggle to progress to the levels we expect of them.

Players struggle to progress because we often forget to teach them the skills that drive self-motivation. So many young players in top academies are wrapped in cotton wool and given everything they want. With low levels of motivation and poor work ethics, they forget why they began playing. They assume they are deserving of things not yet earned. Yes, there are success stories, of course there are, but for every success story (a Rickie Lambert, for example) there are hundreds more young players who fail to see the need to drive their own development and who fall off the scale within a few years.

Motivational Climates (Environments)

Look around the country and you will find a range of professional and amateur clubs that each have a different philosophy, and way of coaching and educating young football players.

Within each club there will be 'that feeling' that echoes around the place; we often term it the footballing environment or club culture. Within this environment, things like discipline, playing style, personality, progression will all develop in different ways. It is in combination that the feeling is created.

Some clubs feel wrong. In fact, too many clubs still feel wrong when it comes to 'winning' at U8 level rather than looking to develop players. They have too many parents shouting and screaming from the touchlines or the team's philosophy is to hoof the ball upfield at every opportunity.

Such environments will often put players off and affect their motivation. Other players' clubs will 'feel' brilliant. They will offer a relaxed, development-oriented environment where performance is put in front of results and parents are cohesive in supporting not only their own children but others (same team and opposition) as well.

These climates/environments can be referred to as either task- or outcome-oriented climates.

A task-oriented climate focuses on the challenge itself and will look to improve individual, unit and team performances before considering the result. Here, mistakes are welcomed and used to educate and not punish players.

An outcome-oriented climate, on the other hand, is more concerned with the result of a game than the performance. Here, mistakes are seen as negative and are punished (often through shouting at a player or subbing them off) and performance style is all about result rather than looking at long-term player development. In such environments, motivation can take a battering, especially with younger age groups where mistakes might be more prevalent and the fear of making mistakes more common.

It is essential that parents and players pick the club (grassroots or academy) that is best for long-term success. As coaches, we must also accept and make clear what environment we will create for teams under our control. Not all parents are going to love or even like what you do, but you should let them know what the 'plan' is.

What environment should coaches be creating?

We all have our own vision of what makes a successful football environment. However, consider the table below when looking to create a suitable environment and ask yourself how you would incorporate appropriate areas to aid development.

Football environments should be	
Safe	Personalised
Fun/Enjoyable	Nurturing
Supportive	Challenging/Progressive
Reflective	Informing
Educating	Honest
Balanced	Diverse

There are, of course, a million-and-one different combinations of what should go into a footballing environment. What is most important, though, is that the child feels that you are there to help them, and to educate them. They should know that you are going to do your very best to develop them.

For me, an environment that looks to develop a growth mindset is one that is conducive to success. Success, here, is the ability of each and every player to play and progress to the very best standard they possibly can. Creating this motivational climate of growth means that you cater for what players want to achieve.

It is important to understand that no player is going to improve if they do not have a particular aim or target to try and achieve. It's why we see learning objectives being used more and more nowadays. Can your environment promote players to set their own learning objectives, and self-motivate? Can you create an environment where personal mastery is at the forefront of a youngster's mind before they have stepped onto the training pitch?

Summary

Ultimately, we all want our young players to grow and develop to the best of their abilities. As such, we need to create an environment that encourages self-motivation in young players. By handing over ownership and a degree of responsibility to young players, we are creating a 'task mastery' environment, which can encourage players to identify and understand the process behind improvement. Here, we are far more likely to see effective development and motivation occur in a number of different situations (football, school, personal).

16. Family, and Friends – How they affect players

The bond that links your true family is not one of blood, but of respect and joy in each other's life.
Richard Bach

As well as parents having a pivotal role in their child's development, a young person will often have key relationships with other family members and close family friends. These relationships often influence what they do. It is therefore essential for families and friends to recognise one another's lives (and dreams/aspirations) and contribute to each other's in turn.

Here are a number of different aspects that family and friends can do to influence young players positively:

1. **Teach** – some family members or close family friends may be knowledgeable and have previous experience of football. For example, there may be past players or coaches who can offer some sound advice.

    What is essential here, however, is that biased opinions do not filter through. For example, we all know someone who stands on the sidelines commenting on how the game should be played. What is extremely important to remember is that there is a huge difference between teaching and educating a young player on the game and facilitating their personal views and opinions.

2. **Guide** – following on from teaching, some family members and friends may be able to offer guidance. They might not have particular answers to issues but will be able to point a young player in the right direction. This might involve showing the player a website or giving them a book to read that aids development (maybe not in football, it might be a book on having fun!). Here the important thing for friends and family to recognise is that it is okay not to know the ins and outs of football, but 'to be there' to guide and point a young player in the right direction.

3. **Support** – As well as teaching and guidance, we can also offer mere support. At times, this is often all that is required. This may be with a player slightly older (12-16 years old) who understands the game, has a good network within football and just needs to general day-to-day interactions (How was training? Did you have fun? What did you learn? etc.). Here we are giving players the opportunity to express themselves on what they have been doing and are able to offer positive reinforcement. Positive support can go a long way in aiding the development of a young player.

4. **Reinforce** – At times, it will be the responsibility of friends and family members to reinforce what others are saying to a young player. This can stem from talking to clubs or having conversations with coaches in relation to playing style, training, effort or even discipline. What is imperative for families to recognise and accept is that sometimes you cannot always defend the player; you must accept what a coach or an employee at the club is saying. This, at times, can be frustrating to do as we all understand that sons and daughters are the centre of a family's universe. However, what must be considered is how advice from coaches and clubs is often the right advice and if you have a clear message to give to young players it is important that parents, family and friends reinforce these points as well.

5. **Perspective** – Finally, a big element to help provide is a bit of perspective. At times, young people can be closed off to listening to their parents, so sometimes it may take an aunt or a cousin to sit a player down, talk to them, and give them a different set of reasons or a different perspective on things. Players will often respond positively to this. Liaising this with family members and understanding the importance of giving different outlooks to young people can help maintain motivation, help players recognise when they are being aided, and provides them with a more open environment to express themselves.

What can family and friends help instil?

By providing the elements above, family and friends have the opportunity to help instil good traits and habits into young players. When examining what clubs and coaches are looking for in players, it can be advantageous to recognise whether some of the following areas are in place or being put in place.

1. **Consistency** – Discussed in chapter 13, the value of consistency in a young person's life is massive when looking at both football and personal development. Family and friends can have a huge impact on instilling a consistent environment for a young player that promotes consistently high standards of attitude, work rate, enthusiasm, motivation, etc.

   This may mean that family and friends know training times, fixtures, and players reports on how they are getting on. Such information can be easily communicated in today's world with emails and text messaging and provides the player with the mindset that everyone is aware of what they are doing (must be kept positive throughout of course) and that people actually care.

2. **Structure** – A clear and effective support structure for a young player is invaluable. This could be as simple as a cousin offering to take a player and a friend to training, players knowing that every two weeks their aunt and uncle

will be coming to watch, or an older brother will be picking them up from training.

3. **Security** – Friends and families that offer consistent support and structure to a young player will be creating a loving and nurturing environment for them to excel and express themselves and provide them with the essential security (especially through the younger age groups (8-11 years old)) that they need in order to progress.

   Often, you will find that players devoid of security display tendencies and behaviours that disrupt and negatively influence others and subsequently affect their own development. It is important for friends and family to liaise with coaches and clubs to allow each party to implement rules and regulations to deal with this. Giving players ownership and reinforcing the security they have can often have a huge impact not only on the player but also on the person.

4. **Options** – Finally, a player who has a network of family and friends is given the option and the encouragement to interact with a variety of people when it comes to football (or life). Here a player may want a different perspective on an issue or maybe a variety of answers so that they can make a decision in relation to training or a game. Here it is important for family and friends to recognise that messages – although they can be put across in different ways – still need to fit within a unified message so that consistency is maintained.

Unity of one message

Following on from the above, what must be recognised (and which is something that I cannot stress enough) is the need for friends and family to be telling the player the same message. What I mean is, not getting caught up in the emotion of things, recognising what is right, and having a player/person understand that doing the right things is essential if progression wants to be seen.

It can be difficult at times for individuals to look beyond their own experiences or see a situation through the eyes of others. I would encourage parents, family and friends to work on this and recognise that they are going to be the most influential set of people that young players will come across (especially in the early years of development).

If friends and family do not see eye-to-eye with coaches, I sincerely believe that it is for the best if there is a parting of ways.

This unity of one message is absolutely essential in delivering consistency for young players to thrive on and build upon.

Summary

If we are looking to have a positive influence on our young players we need to look beyond players, at times, and help educate their parents, family and friends on how much they can help a young player. Through their actions, they are able to help mould and guide young players and help them develop psychologically, emotionally and socially. Simple acts can help players a lot. The importance of showing a unity of message delivered to young players is something that cannot be stressed enough.

17. Developing your own Environment for Success

Be a yardstick of quality. Some people aren't used to an environment where excellence is expected.
Steve Jobs

Throughout this book there have been chapters geared to offer advice and guidance on what it takes to help develop the next generation of young player. Although each piece by itself will offer a young player, coaches, and parents the tools needed to help aid progression, it is really about putting all of this together and creating a sustained environment for success. At present, we often fail to do this on the whole in this country.

Some elite clubs have it, some have had it for years, others are now beginning to develop environments suitable for development in a way that benefits players and clubs, However, if we are to see and instil a change for our national game and the next generation of player we must encourage the development of effective environments throughout the country from grassroots all the way through to academy football.

First define success

Before going on to create an environment of success, you first need to establish what success means to you. Many of us at some point have associated success with winning. Winning is the main thing at the top level; the top teams are there to win trophies and titles. For others though success can mean many different things and what we deem a success must first be deciphered and put out in the open.

Success for the player – When dealing with young players, it may mean parents, family, friends, sitting down with them and talking about what success means to them. At times, don't be surprised if they either don't know what they want to achieve or their main concern is winning a game or scoring a goal. If that is what a young player wants to achieve then fantastic, let them have it.

Some people may, at times, want to steer young players away from initial goals in order to develop them, and this should be fine – but why stop a young player from wanting to win? I believe you can direct them and shape their development with their understanding coming from *why* and *how* to develop. It is not the player's job NOT to want to win or be concerned with winning; it is that competitive edge – at the top level – which is necessary for achievement so don't take that away from them.

Allow the player to write down and tell you what success means to them. Do not put words in their mouth and do not paraphrase what they want. If the player feels they are actively involved in their development (by telling us what they want) then they are much more likely to invest the time and effort to go and succeed. They will persist for longer in the wake of potential setbacks.

Success for the coach – As well as the player needing to define their personal success, coaches need to sit down and think long and hard about why we do what we do, and what success truly means for us.

Here we need to be able to properly evaluate why we are in the positions we are. We will all have different definitions of what success is; some coaches will think about it in terms of personal success (i.e. achieving a first team position at a professional club), others will think about success in the form of how they impact on others (i.e. how many academy players get offered professional contracts or how many grassroots players sign for professional academies). Others, however, may have a much wider view of what success is and what they want to achieve.

At a recent Football League Conference I attended, I was surrounded by academy managers and we were introduced to a performance consultant named Alistair Smith who gave a presentation on 'creating and sustaining a culture for success'. In it, he began by getting everyone to turn to the person next to them and say what success meant for them.

An academy manager turned to me and I blissfully gave my definition of success (so generic and boring), in return I was astounded to hear his, he said (and I paraphrase here) *'I want to leave my mark on football, I want to leave something behind that makes a change and a contribution to the game'*, WOW! I thought it was fantastic to hear someone else so passionate about improving our game for the next generation. As coaches, we are in charge of what we want to achieve. We must recognise and ask ourselves: "what shall we leave behind?"

Success for the club – We can all see the rewards that come from effective definitions of success in professional academies. The likes of Manchester United have embedded what they see as success in their academy for years. Southampton is a more recent example of an academy that has demonstrated the need to develop players. Both Manchester United and Southampton have seen successful in the sense of bringing through youth players into the first team that has led to trophies, transfer profits, and promotions.

What is important for any club at any level is to have a clear vision of what they want to achieve at youth level. Here a club needs to make the use of coaches' experience, trends within football, and honest appraisals to highlight what they want to do going forward. Clubs can then begin to invest in and recruit coaches that follow the same philosophy, style, and culture that they want to see and ultimately create the types of players they are looking for.

Create the culture – Once you have a defined what success means to you and to others (coaches and clubs) you can begin laying essential foundations.

What must be recognised is that it is not just the job of clubs to set this culture out. Individual players can have their own culture, their own way of living their lives to give them the best chance of succeeding in the future. What is imperative I feel is that cultures and environments should look to be created in a range of different settings in order to allow for maximal development to take place.

For the player – So much gets spoken about in relation to clubs developing cultures that help create top young players but what we often forget is that the player is the most important person in this process. So, why not get them to create their own culture within their lives?

At first (especially with younger age groups) this can be difficult (nothing worth doing comes easy, remember!) as the player and person will have quite a heavy reliance on their family on a number of things such as travelling to training and games, diets, sleeping patterns, etc. Here families can have a really positive impact on their child by embedding a structured (but not rigid) routine that will allow the players to excel.

This culture should also look to embed not only football but both personal and academic development in school and out in society. The benefits of this cultural development from a player's perspective are huge and it only really struck me after a conversation I had with a current U18's captain at a Category 1 side. Talking about education and the need to apply himself he came out and said the following: *'I apply myself in football, that's a given for me, so I think why would I change that mentality when I do this (education) work, there's no point in looking at football and education work differently'*. This player, unfortunately, is not archetypal of the majority of players. He attributed his mentality and discipline to his parents and his immediate family. This demonstrates just how influential developing the culture of the player can be and how it can be a positive element for a young player to carry through his early career.

For the coach – Here the development of a culture tends to be a lot more regular. Coaches will generally have what can be seen as a philosophy, a style, and within that, we will generally have a way (a culture) of how they want things done, both in training and in games.

Coaches can have another huge impact on young players by creating and selling a culture aimed at personal and professional development. As well as the playing styles, the roles and responsibilities on the pitch, coaches can have rules and etiquette before and after training and games; most clubs have the policy of players shaking hands with the coach before and after training and games, but how many coaches actually ask their players to shake hands with one another? A simple mark of respect to one another.

Other basic cultural policies can include allocating individuals to bring equipment to and from the lock ups or coaches' cars, and changing this weekly or monthly. Another development exercise I have seen some excellent coaches do is to allow players to run their warm up, and not just the captain, a goalkeeper or the quiet player taking a full warm up and encouraging players to respect and listen to what they are being asked to do.

With these basic cultures brought in you will find attention to detail of what can be seen as the 'little things' becoming habit (hand shaking among players, warm ups). These habits mean players are going to pay more attention to warm ups seeing as they know they will be required to carry one out (or a cool down for example); they will begin to recognise the reasoning behind why they are done and can develop understanding which is positive for their development.

As coaches, ask yourself the questions related to culture, what are you giving the players on top of their football techniques, in a fun, nurturing environment? What more can you give to help develop the person as well?

For the club – For clubs cultural development is probably the most important aspect of player development (whether the aim is to sell a player on to make profit or to put them into the first team).

The culture of a club (especially at youth level) defines who you are, what you are all about, and that stretches way beyond the football field.

Clubs (at any level) would need to sit down and thrash out topics such as core values, what success is, playing style, organisation, etc., This may take some time but the potential rewards from actively taking responsibility for developing an environment where everyone feels part of it (and where everyone feels they can be successful) is so important.

Take the example of the New Zealand rugby union team. In the book *Legacy* by James Kerr followed and observed the new regime of the New Zealand rugby team and documented how the management team transformed a side that had suffered a string of bad results and a loss of identity into a side that dominated international rugby.

The book presented 15 key lessons to take in leadership, which came from management and revolved around the importance of creating a culture of success and of achievement. Within football, we can take a lot from those lessons and some clubs have implemented similar cultures for years (the Uniteds, Crewe, Southampton, Barcelona, etc.). They reap the rewards because of the structure and organisation put in place.

What we must recognise is that involving the right people in the right areas is crucial and clubs can no longer simply hire a 'mate', a past player just because they know them. We are no longer in a position of power in English football that allows us to be so naïve and we need to make the hiring process just as much a part of our cultural and environmental development as anything else.

So there are things that we can all do to help create and sustain a culture of success; we each have a part to play if we are going to make a difference and leave a lasting legacy on the English game.

Set the Standards

Once you are aware of what success is, and you have a clear outline of the type of culture you wish to create, you will begin to have an idea about standards. Here setting standards for the next generation is fundamental to establishing and continuing success. These standards come in many forms.

Clubs and coaches should sit down and discuss standards, the important thing being that all standards should be linked and built into the philosophy that the club has created (or which it is creating). Core values and beliefs should be demonstrated and put into these standards.

The inclusion of respect, politeness, and discipline should be intertwined with club rules and regulations, as well as the idea of players in each age group providing their own rules and regulations for the season. Here coaches can encourage ownership and responsibility.

Importantly, standards must be raised through the age groups for aspects outside football. Things like maintaining good reports in schools and obtaining reports from parents can be part and parcel of the standards that players need to demonstrate.

Have a support network established

Having established what success is, the culture of the club, and a sound set of operating standards as the foundation for player development, they now have to be communicated effectively to everyone that has involvement within the club. From management through to lunch ladies, cleaners, and volunteers should all be aware of what is being created. Once personnel are fully aware of what the club is creating and what they stand for then you can begin to filter this information through to parents and players.

Coaches (in elite football this can be lead phase coaches and academy managers) should communicate what the club is about at the beginning of the season, in club meetings, make use of technology (emails) and via social media (Facebook, twitter). This can often be highly effective as you find parents and guardians working late nowadays. They can struggle to get to meetings in person so the use of technology should be varied and as accessible as possible.

Making players and their families aware of all of this can provide an effective support network for the player should they feel help is needed. Contacts for personnel such as coaches, welfare officers, education officers (in elite football) or volunteers, club chairman's/presidents, etc. (in grassroots football) can be used. As players get older, and habits are created, they can gain access to this support network without the involvement of parents.

Summary

However we choose to define success, what we want our culture to be, and what standards we want to set, will ultimately drive the next generation of player.

It is essential that footballing organisations (The F.A.), elite clubs, grassroots clubs, coaches, parents and players themselves see the value in the need for creating and sustaining a culture of success. This success must be defined and refined in order to maintain standards and these must be effectively communicated to all.

Epilogue

Bringing this book's chapters together has, I hope, given some insight into the need to develop better people if we want to help develop and create the next generation of football player. The game has changed and so has our society and youth. As such, we must move with those times in many ways to allow for the evolution of the sport, its teams, and its players.

When it comes to the footballing side, we have an enormous number of resources at our disposal that allow us to generate coaching sessions to aid development. We also have some outstanding coaches that work within the system.

But more can be done.

I would like to see football have a greater influence on young people. In a recent coaches' meeting, the academy manager made reference to the fact that 'we', as coaches, only have about 4% of a young person's time during a 7 day week and that it is important we make the most of that 4%. Although it was suggested that a club and coach can have little influence over everything else (home life, education, personal development) – I disagree.

Here is where 'we' *can* make a big difference! We can instil elements and examples from the book into young people's lives so that they can not only handle the technical and tactical demands of their sport but also deal with the highs and lows of success and failure. By taking a holistic view into the person and player combined, we can help them to deal with adversity, not let them lose sight of their identity, and recognise their strengths to pursue greatness in other ways.

I am not saying this book has all the answers, if anything it probably offers more in the way of questions and considerations, but I am firm in my beliefs that by having a positive impact on the young person, by helping support parents and schools, we can create a new generation of person able to not only cope with the football industry but life as it is today.

Other Books from Bennion Kearny

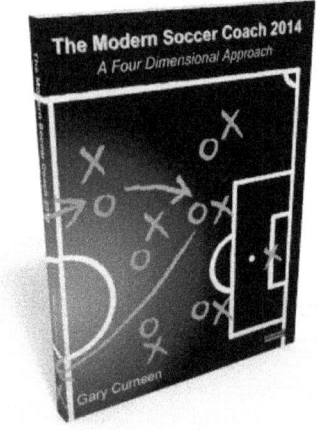

The Modern Soccer Coach by Gary Curneen

Aimed at Soccer coaches of all levels and with players of all ages and abilities The Modern Soccer Coach 2014 identifies the areas that must be targeted by coaches who want to maximize a team's potential – the Technical, Tactical, Physical, and Mental sides to the game. See how the game has changed and what areas determine success in the game today. Learn what sets coaches like Mourinho, Klopp, Rodgers, and Guardiola apart from the rest. Philosophies and training methods from the most forward thinking coaches in the game today are presented, along with guidelines on creating a modern environment for readers' teams. This book is not about old school methodologies – it is about creating a culture of excellence that gets the very best from players. Contains more than 30 illustrated exercises that focus on tactical, technical, mental, and physical elements of the game.

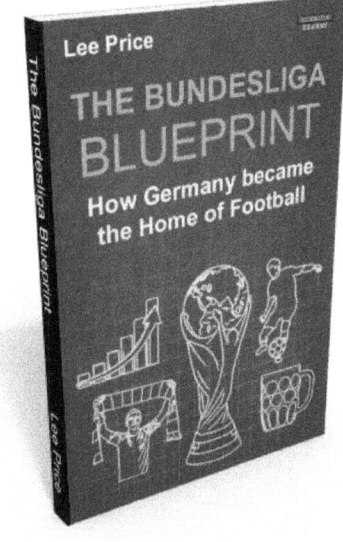

The Bundesliga Blueprint: How Germany became the Home of Football by Lee Price

In this entertaining, fascinating, and superbly-researched book, sportswriter Lee Price explores German football's 10-year plan. A plan that forced clubs to invest in youth, limit the number of foreign players in teams, build success without debt, and much more. The Bundesliga Blueprint details how German fans part-own and shape their clubs, how football is affordable, and the value of beer and a good sausage on match days. The book includes interviews from Michael Ballack, Jens Nowotny and Christoph Kramer, and the movers-and-shakers behind Germany's leading clubs including Schalke, Dortmund, and Paderborn.

Soccer Tough: Simple Football Psychology Techniques to Improve Your Game by Dan Abrahams

"Take a minute to slip into the mind of one of the world's greatest soccer players and imagine a stadium around you. Picture a performance under the lights and mentally play the perfect game."

Technique, speed and tactical execution are crucial components of winning soccer, but it is mental toughness that marks out the very best players – the ability to play when pressure is highest, the opposition is strongest, and fear is greatest. Top players and coaches understand the importance of sport psychology in soccer but how do you actually train your mind to become the best player you can be? Soccer Tough demystifies this crucial side of the game and offers practical techniques that will enable soccer players of all abilities to actively develop focus, energy, and confidence. Soccer Tough will help banish the fear, mistakes, and mental limits that holds players back.

The Way Forward: Solutions to England's Football Failings
by Matthew Whitehouse

In his acclaimed book, The Way Forward, football coach Matthew Whitehouse examines the causes of English football's decline and offers a number of areas where change and improvement need to be implemented immediately. With a keen focus and passion for youth development and improved coaching he explains that no single fix can overcome current difficulties and that a multi-pronged strategy is needed. If we wish to improve the standards of players in England then we must address the issues in schools, the grassroots, and academies, as well as looking at the constraints of the Premier League and English FA.

Scientific Approaches to Goalkeeping in Football: A practical perspective on the most unique position in sport
by Andy Elleray

Do you coach goalkeepers and want to help them realise their fullest potential? Are you a goalkeeper looking to reach the top of your game? Then search no further and dive into this dedicated goalkeeping resource. Written by goalkeeping guru Andy Elleray this book offers a fresh and innovative approach to goalkeeping in football. With a particular emphasis on the development of young goalkeepers, it sheds light on training, player development, match performances, and player analysis. Utilising his own experiences Andy shows the reader various approaches, systems and exercises that will enable goalkeepers to train effectively and appropriately to bring out the very best in them.

The Modern Soccer Coach: Position-Specific Training by Gary Curneen

Aimed at football coaches of all levels, and players of all ages and abilities, The Modern Soccer Coach: Position-Specific Training seeks to identify, develop, and enhance the skills and functions of the modern soccer player whatever their position and role on the pitch.

This book offers unique insight into how to develop an elite program that can both improve players and win games. Filled with practical no-nonsense explanations, focused player drills, and more than 40 illustrated soccer templates, this book will help you – the modern coach - to create a coaching environment that will take your players to the next level.

The Footballer's Journey: real-world advice on becoming and remaining a professional footballer by Dean Caslake and Guy Branston

Many youngsters dream of becoming a professional footballer. But football is a highly competitive world where only a handful will succeed. Many aspiring soccer players don't know exactly what to expect, or what is required, to make the transition from the amateur world to the 'bright lights' in front of thousands of fans. The Footballer's Journey maps out the footballer's path with candid insight and no-nonsense advice. It examines the reality of becoming a footballer including the odds of 'making it', how academies really work, the importance of attitude and mindset, and even the value of having a backup plan if things don't quite work out.

Making The Ball Roll: A Complete Guide to Youth Football for the Aspiring Soccer Coach by Ray Power

Making the Ball Roll is the ultimate complete guide to coaching youth soccer.

This focused and easy-to-understand book details training practices and tactics, and goes on to show you how to help young players achieve peak performance through tactical preparation, communication, psychology, and age-specific considerations. Each chapter covers, in detail, a separate aspect of coaching to give you, the football coach, a broad understanding of youth soccer development. Each topic is brought to life by the stories of real coaches working with real players. Never before has such a comprehensive guide to coaching soccer been found in the one place. If you are a new coach, or just trying to improve your work with players - and looking to invest in your future - this is a must-read book!

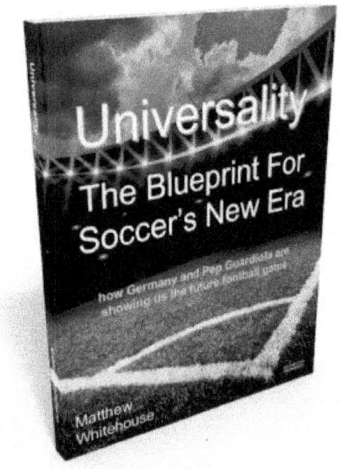

Universality | The Blueprint for Soccer's New Era: How Germany and Pep Guardiola are showing us the Future Football Game by Matthew Whitehouse

The game of soccer is constantly in flux; new ideas, philosophies and tactics mould the present and shape the future. In this book, Matthew Whitehouse – acclaimed author of The Way Forward: Solutions to England's Football Failings - looks in-depth at the past decade of the game, taking the reader on a journey into football's evolution. Examining the key changes that have occurred since the turn of the century, right up to the present, the book looks at the evolution of tactics, coaching, and position-specific play. They have led us to this moment: to the rise of universality. Universality | The Blueprint For Soccer's New Era is a voyage into football, as well as a lesson for coaches, players and fans who seek to know and anticipate where the game of the future is heading.

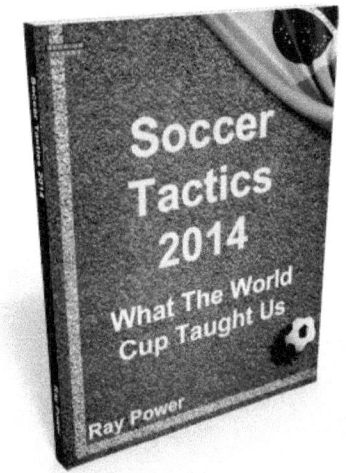

Soccer Tactics 2014: What The World Cup Taught Us by Ray Power

World Cups throw up unique tactical variations. Countries and football cultures from around the globe converge, in one place, to battle it out for world soccer supremacy. The 2014 World Cup in Brazil was no different, arguably throwing up tactical differences like never seen at a competition in modern times. Contests are not just won by strong work ethics and technical brilliance, but by tactical discipline, fluidity, effective strategies, and (even) unique national traits. Soccer Tactics 2014 analyses the intricacies of modern international systems, through the lens of matches in Brazil. Covering formations, game plans, key playing positions, and individuals who bring football tactics to life - the book offers analysis and insights for soccer coaches, football players, and fans the world over. The book sheds light on where football tactics currently stand… and where they are going. Includes analysis of group matches, knock out stages, and the final.

Developing the Modern Footballer through Futsal by Michael Skubala and Seth Burkett

Aimed at coaches of all levels and ages, Developing the Modern Footballer through Futsal is a concise and practical book that provides an easy-to-understand and comprehensive guide to the ways in which futsal can be used as a development tool for football. From defending and attacking to transitional play and goalkeeping, this book provides something for everyone and aims to get you up-and-running fast.

Over 50 detailed sessions are provided, with each one related to specific football scenarios and detailing how performance in these scenarios can be improved through futsal. From gegenpressing to innovative creative play under pressure, this book outlines how futsal can be used to develop a wide range of football-specific skills, giving your players the edge.

Deliberate Soccer Practice: 50 Passing & Possession Football Exercises to Improve Decision-Making by Ray Power

Aimed at football coaches of all levels, but with a particular emphasis on coaches who work with youth players, *50 Passing & Possession Football Exercises to Improve Decision-Making* is comprised of 20 Technical Practices and 30 Possession Practices. They are carefully designed to be adaptable to suit the needs of the players you work with; to challenge them and give them decisions to make. The sessions look to make soccer complex and realistically difficult – no passing in queues from one cone to the next with no interference. Crucially, the exercises offer a means to accelerate player development effectively and enjoyably.

Other Recent Books from Bennion Kearny

Tipping The Balance: The Mental Skills Handbook For Athletes
by Dr Martin Turner & Dr Jamie Barker

The 7 Master Moves of Success
by Jag Shoker

**Paul Webb Academy: Strength Training Books
for Footballers and Goalkeepers**

Learn More about our Books at:

www.BennionKearny.com/Soccer

www.ingramcontent.com/pod-product-compliance
Lightning Source LLC
Chambersburg PA
CBHW081229170426
43191CB00036B/2328